CHRISTIAN EDUCATION IN THE SMALL CHURCH

CHRISTIAN EDUCATION IN THE SMALL CHURCH

DONALD L. GRIGGS

JUDY McKAY WALTHER

Judson Press® Valley Forge

CHRISTIAN EDUCATION IN THE SMALL CHURCH

Copyright © 1988
Judson Press, Valley Forge, PA 19482-0851

Second Printing, 1988

Bible quotations in this volume are from

HOLY BIBLE New International Version, copyright © 1978, New York International Bible Society. Used by permission.

Good News Bible, the Bible in Today's English Version. Copyright © American Bible Society, 1976. Used by permission

Library of Congress Cataloging-in-Publication Data
Griggs, Donald L.
  Christian education in the small church.

  (Small church in action)
    1. Christian education.   2. Small churches.
  I. Walther, Judy McKay.   II. Walrath, Douglas Alan,
  1933–   III. Title.   IV. Series.
  BV1471.2.G675   1988   268   87-35792
  ISBN 0-8170-1103-X

Contents

84228

Foreword

Small churches are in a class by themselves. To overlook that uniqueness is to misunderstand them.

Unfortunately, small churches are commonly misunderstood. For example, they have long been viewed as proving grounds for new pastors. According to that assumption, beginning pastors should make their mistakes in small churches; fewer people are involved, and therefore the mistakes will be less costly. Also, those who demonstrate their ability in ministry with small churches will likely be effective pastors of larger churches.

Such viewpoints are hardly warranted. Only the most crass perspective could hold that those who are members of small churches deserve consistently lower quality, less experienced pastoral care than those who are members of large churches. Small churches are not smaller versions of large churches. They are qualitatively, as well as quantitatively, different. Nor do the insights that pastors gain in ministry with small congregations transfer directly to larger congregations. In my own experience, those who minister well and are happy in small churches rarely are as happy or effective when they move to large churches. Church members who are nurtured and who are effective lay leaders in small churches rarely find similar nurture or are as able to serve when those small churches become larger.

Small churches deserve to be dealt with in their own right. Denominational programs in education, outreach, and stewardship that are designed for large churches rarely suit the needs of small congregations. To draw the potential out of small congregations, those who lead them and who provide resources for them need to appreciate their potential as small churches.

This series of books is designed specifically for those who lead and support small churches. Each author is someone who cares about and understands the unique possibilities of small congregations.

Some years ago after a conference on Christian education, a participant shared his frustration. While he now knew what Christian education should be, he didn't see how he could implement what he had learned at the conference in the small church where he served. None of the methods and resources to which he had been introduced were suitable for use in small congregations.

The story relates an experience that is familiar to most of us who serve as leaders of small churches. But that all-too-familiar experience is *not* repeated in the pages ahead.

In *Christian Education in the Small Church,* Don Griggs and Judy Walther write especially to meet the needs of those who guide Christian education in small churches. This book is full of practical ideas and suggestions designed specifically for those who engage in Christian education in small congregations.

Both authors are well equipped to speak to the needs of those who engage in Christian education in small churches. For many years Don Griggs has prepared pastors and laypersons to be effective leaders in all phases of Christian education. Both his teaching and writing are highly regarded. Judy Walther brings a wealth of insight gained from hands-on experience as a pastor of small churches and more recently as a staff person concerned with supporting leaders of small churches. Their book offers sound theory and workable methods that will be useful to all who carry on the ministry of education in small churches.

Douglas Alan Walrath
Strong, Maine

Introduction

Christian education is a central element of the ministry of every church. It is in and through the educational ministry of the church that men and women and boys and girls are enabled to hear, experience, and put into practice the teachings of Jesus and of the sages, prophets, apostles, and saints of all the generations of the church's heritage. In Psalm 78 the psalmist speaks for the teachers of every age:

> I am going to use wise sayings
>   and explain mysteries from the past,
>   things we have heard and known,
>   things that our fathers told us.
> We will not keep them from our children;
>   we will tell the next generation
>   about the LORD's power and his great deeds
>   and the wonderful things he has done.
> He gave laws to the people of Israel
>   and commandments to the descendants of Jacob.
> He instructed our ancestors
>   to teach his laws to their children,
> so that the next generation might learn them
>   and in turn should tell their children.

> In this way they also will put their trust in God
> and not forget what he has done,
> but always obey his commandments.
> —Psalm 78:2–7(TEV)

In small and large churches, in city and rural churches, in well established and new churches, in churches everywhere, the challenge is the same—to present the gospel of Jesus Christ in ways that are compelling and memorable so that persons of all ages and circumstances will be nurtured in the Christian faith in order to be empowered to live faithfully as disciples of Jesus Christ. Even though we live and serve in an age of supersonic transportation and instantaneous worldwide communication, some of the essential needs of people are the same as they always have been. Each person needs to discover what it means to be created in the image of God and named a child of God, to develop relationships of love that are mutually fulfilling, to know who God is and what God intends for one's future, and to work for peace and justice in the world. In our day the church may be one of the only places where these needs have a chance of being fulfilled. Especially in the smaller church there are many opportunities for persons to build significant relationships, to learn how to live and serve faithfully as disciples of Christ, and to share together a vision of what God desires for the created order.

This book is written on the premise that Christian education is not only an important program of the church but also a way to influence and permeate all other aspects of the church's ministry. Chapter 1 seeks to articulate this understanding of Christian education by explaining that more is involved in Christian education than organizing a good church school and popular youth fellowship. In Chapter 2 we give attention to the variety of settings in which smaller churches find themselves. The setting of a church greatly influences the specific goals, programs, and approaches to ministry appropriate to the church and the community that it serves. The effectiveness of a church's educational ministry depends upon the leaders who are responsible for all the various programs and emphases. Chapters 3, 4, and 5 explore in depth the many aspects of leadership development, nurture, and support.

All educational programs, classes, and groups that meet in order to study, discuss, and share the heritage of their Christian faith need materials and resources to guide the teachers, leaders, and participants. In Chapter 6 there is an emphasis on curriculum; however, curriculum is presented in a way that moves beyond thinking of just printed materials. A way of determining goals for Christian education and developing criteria for evaluating curriculum is outlined in a step-by-step process. In addition to curriculum there is need to consider the place of facilities, equipment, and resources as elements that affect the quality of Christian education in a church. That is the focus for Chapter 7. The book concludes with a chapter that presents a very practical way for building the relationship between worship and Christian education.

Between them the authors bring to their writing more than fifty years of experience in Christian education. Donald Griggs has served as a Christian educator for two churches and as a professor of Christian education in a theological school and is an author of a number of Christian education resources. Don has led many continuing education events for pastors and Christian education workshops for teachers of smaller churches. It is out of that variety of experience that Don has written Chapters 1, 4, 5, and 6. Judy McKay Walther has served as a pastor of several smaller churches, most recently as the organizing pastor of a new church. Presently Judy is working as a regional staff person, serving as a resource person and consultant to many small churches in Idaho and eastern Oregon. From the context of her many years of work in and with smaller churches, Judy has written

Chapters 2, 3, 7, and 8. In Chapter 8 Judy writes very personally about her experiences of trying to build bridges between worship and education for persons of all ages.

Both authors write with the conviction that the total life and ministry of every church can be influenced by pastors and church leaders when they adopt an educational approach and style in their work. In very positive ways they can work to accomplish the goals set forth by Jesus when he told his followers, "Go and make disciples of all nations, baptizing them in the name of the Father and of the Son and of the Holy Spirit, and teaching them to obey everything I have commanded you" (Matthew 28:19-20, NIV). Jesus has promised that he will be with us always, to the very end of the age. When we live with that confidence and hope and when we seek to be faithful to the ministry to which each one of us has been called and gifted, we will take our place among the faithful of every generation who have been the bearers of the Good News and the teachers of "wise sayings, mysteries from the past, and the LORD's power and great deeds."

Christian Education Is More Than Sunday Church School

A visitor to church asks, "Tell me about the Christian education program in your church." Where do you begin as you seek to describe the Christian education program of the church where you minister and are a member? As we have traveled and visited with pastors and leaders, we have asked many persons to tell us about Christian education in their churches. Their responses follow a familiar pattern. The first thing that is mentioned is the church school that meets on Sunday mornings. Usually the focus of the church school is on what happens with the children. Often pastors will suggest that we speak with other persons in the church who know more than they do about what is happening in Christian education. There are many occasions when persons will describe an event such as vacation church school, day camp, an Advent festival, or some other special program. Even though all of the responses do provide a little information, they present a very limiting view of Christian education.

If Christian education is seen primarily as a children's program on Sunday mornings, plus some special events throughout the year that are planned and led by the church's members without much involvement of the pastor, then Christian education will never be able to fulfill its potential as a ministry that is able to undergird, nurture, and expand the whole ministry of the church. It is important for Christian education to be perceived from a more inclusive and wholistic view, especially in the smaller church, where members and pastor must assume a variety of roles and responsibilities in the church's many faceted ministries. In this regard the smaller church may have an advantage over larger churches because it is easier to gain a more wholistic perspective. Yet, many smaller churches fall into the same trap as their larger neighbors by relegating Christian education to a narrow, limited place in the life of the church. In order to become more effective in serving the total ministry of the church, it is necessary to adjust some of the ways we think about and approach doing Christian education.

It is essential that Christian education be seen as more than programs for children. It is natural to focus on the children. As parents and adults, we desire for our children to learn the heritage of their faith and to grow into faithful, believing Christians. Being responsible parents, we arrange for music lessons, recreational activities, and other special events that provide for the care and nurture of our children. We also plan for their education in the church by providing a church school and other programs that contribute to their Christian nurture.

There is nothing wrong with this emphasis on the children. In fact, we would be less than responsible if we did not provide such programs. However, we are mistaken when we limit our vision of, and commitment to, what Christian education should and can be by concentrating on what the children need and what we can do for them. Church school thus becomes identified primarily as a children's program.

Young adolescents are by nature working their way through the complex path from childhood to adulthood so that by the time they enter junior high school, many of them feel that they have outgrown church school. If church school is for children, then one way for them to declare that they are no longer children is to stop attending church school. They find all kinds of excuses not to attend. And it is difficult for many parents to insist that their adolescent children go to church school when the parents themselves do not see this as an important aspect of their own Christian nurture.

As important as Christian education for children and youth is, I believe that the measure of an effective, responsible educational ministry is what is happening for and among the adults. Regardless of the size of the congregation, there are usually many more adults associated with the church than there are children and youth. That would suggest that there should be more programs of Christian education offered for adults than there are for children and youth. Yet, the opposite is usually the case; there are more classrooms, more programs, more teachers, more money, and more commitment to Christian education focused on children and youth than on adults. This is indicative of the premise with which we started: Christian education is often perceived as a children's program. Learning what it means to be Christian, learning the Bible and its relevance for daily faith and life, learning about the needs of people and ways to respond to those needs, and learning to love God, neighbor, and self is a lifelong process. For these, and many more reasons, adults need quality educational experiences as much as the children and youth need them.

It is essential that Christian education be offered at times in addition to Sunday. Church school and worship in the morning and youth fellowship groups in the evening are great opportunities for providing Christian education. These are the traditional times and programs that serve as a foundation for whatever Christian education is developed. However, to limit Christian education to Sunday is to fail to see the many other times and settings during the week that present themselves as excellent opportunities for nurture and growth in the Christian faith.

A midweek evening when a small group of adults spends two hours together will provide not only more time for in-depth study of the Bible but also more time to build relationships among the members of the group. There are excellent resources available for in-depth Bible study from denominational sources and from others such as the Kerygma Program, Bethel Bible Series, Trinity Bible Studies, and many more. Churches of all sizes that have instituted such programs report significant changes in the lives of persons as well as in the life of the congregation. A pastor serving a new church of seventy-four members reports that more than twenty-five adults have completed *Kerygma: Bible Study In-Depth.* Most of the church officers participated. The pastor describes the difference this has made in the ways persons hear sermons, respond to issues, plan for teaching, and speak about the Bible. In a second offering of the program, another fifteen to twenty persons plan to participate.

A midweek early morning gathering for breakfast, fellowship, Bible study, and prayer could be planned as part of the educational program for adults. Such gatherings become very important in the lives of those who attend when there is careful attention given to planning, building relationships, and making the meetings worthwhile for those who attend. In one small church there are ten men who meet every Wednesday for breakfast at a coffee shop where a side room is reserved for them. The pastor is present and takes the lead in the Bible study by sharing a passage of Scripture and then asking questions to get the discussion going. The men all feel free to ask their own questions, to express themselves candidly, and to share from the depths of their experiences. One man in the group testifies that his week, and his life, would be empty without the fellowship he experiences each Wednesday morning with his pastor and other fellow members.

Some churches have discovered that a program on one Saturday each month provides for significant enrichment of their educational programs. Families in churches of all sizes often have difficulty maintaining regular attendance on Sunday mornings. A Saturday program for four to five hours once a month provides time for such activities as Bible study, recreation, a meal, informal worship, a service project, and music. When nine or ten Saturdays of the year are scheduled in advance, families and individuals are able to plan their own schedules in order to include these special programs as part of their commitment to the church's program. Teachers and leaders who may not be available on a weekly basis are more able and willing to serve in such a program. A Saturday program of Christian education for children, youth, and adults would not necessarily replace the weekly Sunday church school; rather it would be a supplement to it.

Supplemental Saturday programs are one way of increasing time for quality Christian education. Nine to ten Saturdays per year would double the amount of time that most persons usually spend in church school in the same year. Four to five hours of a focused, well-planned program would also demonstrate that learning about and being Christian involves more than attending a class to study the Bible. Such study becomes integrated with other activities that provide variety and wholeness to the program.

When several leaders and planners in a church see the potential for doing Christian education at other times in addition to Sunday morning or evening, they will discover times, settings, and formats that are especially appropriate to their situation. The primary prerequisites for developing such programs are commitment to the validity of the idea and willingness to spend the time and energy necessary to make it happen.

It is essential that the pastor be involved in the planning and leadership of the Christian education program. From its beginning the Sunday church school has been an institution that has, in most churches, depended upon the support and leadership of the officers and members of the church, rather than the pastors. Combining that historical note with the reality that in their theological education most pastors receive no, or very little, training in the area of Christian education, it is not surprising that they feel ill equipped to help plan and support the Christian education program of their churches. They are more than willing to encourage the members and officers to take major responsibility for planning and leading the educational programs. Given the many responsibilities and demands upon the time of the pastor, it is natural for the pastor to be satisfied that others are taking care of the Christian education program. When pastors allow the Christian education activities of the church to happen without their direct involvement, they are missing one of the best opportunities available for the nurture, care, and support of all the members of their congregations. Many reports indicate that the growing churches are not always the ones that are aggressive in their outreach programs, but rather are the ones that emphasize quality and diversity in their education programs as they respond to the needs and interests of all the members and age groups of their constituency.

It is not likely that the curriculum of theological education will change soon in order to equip pastors with better educational perspectives and teaching skills. However, there are many things that pastors can do to increase their effectiveness in the educational ministries of the church. The first and most critical step is for pastors to give Christian education a higher priority in terms of the churches' various programs as well as in terms of their own commitments of time and energy. Other steps include reading helpful books, subscribing to and reading one or two periodicals devoted to Christian education, meeting periodically with pastors or church educators from nearby churches to discuss their mutual concerns about Christian education, and attending occasional continuing education events, conferences, or workshops where Christian education topics will be featured. In addition, pastors can work at implementing the key educational principles that are described in what follows. All of these would be helpful, significant steps that would influence beyond measure the Christian education programs of their churches.

It is essential that sound educational principles be applied to all aspects of the church's ministry and not just to traditional Christian education programs. When the pastor and key leaders are committed to intentional application of several foundational educational principles, it is possible for them to make a positive impact upon many of the church's programs and activities. What follows is a list of five significant representative educational principles and some examples of how they may be applied to worship services, study classes, fellowship groups, committee meetings, and other gatherings of church members.

Concepts that are concrete can be communicated more easily than abstract concepts. Jesus illustrated this principle very well through his use of parables, actions, and relationships in which the common, ordinary "stuff" of life provided the images and vocabulary for communicating about abstract concepts such as forgiveness, the kingdom of God, righteousness, justice, faithfulness, and other aspects of life lived in obedience to God's will. His actions and teachings were, and are, memorable because persons were able to connect with them in terms of their own life experiences. Pastors and leaders must ask themselves an important question

21

when they are planning and leading worship, classes, meetings, and other gatherings: "How can we reduce the abstractions of prayers, sermons, teaching activities, and agendas for meetings in order to relate what we seek to communicate to the experiences of those whom we lead, teach, and guide?" When our vocabulary, the images we use, and the stories we tell are relevant to those who are present, we will not only communicate better but the people will also be able to appropriate for themselves what we seek to share with them.

Persons who are offered choices are more motivated to participate and learn than persons who are not given choices. It seems to be an axiom of human nature that we are more motivated by elective courses than we are by required courses. It is important to offer choices to participants because persons have different interests, needs, and abilities. They learn in different ways, and they perceive reality differently from one another. When persons are provided the opportunity to choose from among alternatives, several things are communicated.

- The leader suggests there is more than one acceptable way to think, believe, or act.
- Participants are free to choose based upon their personal interests, feelings, values, and ideas.
- Participants have an "investment" in the process and begin to care about the activity, the project, the discussion, or whatever is happening.
- There is an affirmation of persons as ones who are capable of being responsible for the choices they make.
- There is a variety of points of view expressed and actions taken so that the whole group benefits from the diverse contributions of everyone.

There are many significant as well as subtle ways that this principle is implemented in the various programs of the church. Teachers ask open-ended questions for which there are many appropriate answers. Teachers offer more than one way to share interpretations of Bible passages. Such activities include speaking, writing, dramatizing, drawing, or singing, not all in one session but over a period of time. Leaders of committees encourage the members to consider alternative ways to solve problems or to offer programs. Persons are invited to decide which committee to serve on, which class to attend, or which task to do from among two or more alternatives. In a sermon the pastor presents at least two ways of interpreting a passage or several ways to act on what one believes. These and dozens of other possibilities are all examples of implementing this basic educational principle.

Dialogue produces more learning and growth than monologue. When the congregation mostly listens to a pastor reading, praying, and preaching, there is not much opportunity for dialogue. When a class mostly listens to a teacher explaining, telling, and interpreting, there is not much opportunity for dialogue. When a committee mostly listens to a leader telling them what will happen, there is not much opportunity for dialogue. Pastors, teachers, and leaders must first be committed to the principle that dialogue contributes more to learning than monologue. Then their next step is to devise ways to introduce the element of dialogue in the various settings where they lead others.

For example, without any radical changes in the order of worship, there are several ways to introduce a little dialogue into a setting that by design is usually more conducive to monologue.

- A small group could meet on a midweek evening with the pastor for Bible study focused on the texts for the sermons for the next four to six weeks. In addition to the dialogue that takes place during the study, the members of the group can continue in dialogue even during the sermons as they interact in their own minds with what they are hearing.

- The worshipers could be invited to offer their own prayers of thanksgiving, intercession, and petition.
- Before or after singing a hymn, the congregation could spend a few moments in silence, or in dialogue, responding to a question such as "As you read or sing the words of the hymn, what affirmations of faith are expressed for you in some of those words?"
- There could be blank cards in the pews or space in the bulletin for persons to write messages prompted by what is happening in worship. These messages could be directed to the pastor or the church officers or a specific committee.
- Included in the bulletin could be a series of three or more questions, different each week, that invite the worshipers to reflect on and respond to the sermon or any other part of the service.
- If there are Bibles in the pews, the worshipers could be invited to read the Scripture as it is read from the pulpit and then to spend a few moments in silence meditating on the passage after it has been read.

Persons care more about what happens when they are able to commit themselves to tangible, meaningful tasks. When there are relatively few individuals to do many tasks, as is true in smaller churches, it is important for every person to assume his or her part of the ministry of the church. We are accustomed to asking persons to commit themselves in the context of worship. They are asked to commit their time, their money, and their abilities. Often the commitments are called for in general ways so that those who hear the invitation to commitment respond in general ways by assenting to what they hear without acting on it. Specific needs, problems, or opportunities should be identified, with suggestions of specific ways to make commitments so that persons will know clearly how they may be able to respond.

In one church a special dinner is prepared every Christmas Eve for persons who are alone. Many come to the church for the meal and the early family worship service. Many others who cannot leave their homes receive a meal that is delivered to them. It takes a large cadre of persons to tend to all the details. Instead of just asking for volunteers through general announcements, a small poster is prepared with all of the tasks listed and a space for someone to sign-up for each specific task. If five dishwashers are needed, there are five blank spaces; and so it is with each task. Every year the whole list is completed without much extra effort. One of the reasons for such success is that individuals are presented with specific tasks and are able to choose the ones they feel able to do.

A committee meeting should not end without all members having specific responsibilities and knowing what is expected of them between one meeting and the next. One reason meetings are often unproductive is that decisions are not made and strategies not agreed to regarding what persons are committed to do for the next meeting or what will happen between the meetings.

A Bible study class is not complete without inviting participants to relate what they are studying in the Bible to their own lives and faith journeys. There need to be questions for discussion and other learning activities that encourage class members to struggle with the meaning of the biblical texts in terms of their own needs, problems, and responsibilities.

We have tried to suggest in this chapter that Christian education is more than Sunday church school. Christian education is for all ages and especially for adults. Christian education can happen at other times in addition to Sunday. The pastor is a key person in the educational ministry of the church, and with some reordering of priorities and perceptions, the pastor can serve effectively as part of the team of educational leaders in the church. Also, there are some very basic educational principles which when consciously understood and conscientiously implemented can make a significant impact upon the whole ministry of the church. All of what we have suggested must be considered in light of the particular setting in which a church finds itself. The historical, cultural, social, geographical, and demographic setting in which a church finds itself will influence greatly the extent to which it is able to revise older programs or to consider implementing new approaches for Christian education.

2

Developing Christian Education Where You Live

Congregations are located in communities and are made up of people whose lives are affected by the social settings in which they live. Consequently, when we speak of small churches, we speak of variety. The development of effective educational ministries in small churches is related to the ability of the congregations to look at themselves, to discover the needs that must be addressed, and to find ways to communicate the gospel among themselves and to those who live in their communities. Each congregation must begin to see its educational ministry as specialized, tailored for the particular time and place in which it lives.

Most denominations have produced studies on the small church, and several individuals have written helpful books that categorize types of small churches. Jackson Carroll, Carl Dudley, Lyle Schaller, Doug Walrath, and others have helped us to see that churches have personalities and lifestyles that are related to location, history, age, self-image, and sense of mission. A congregation that wishes to evaluate its Christian education ministry would benefit from reading some of these basic resources and developing a description of its congregational life before changing or developing any programs. Such a description might include the features of the congregation that are valued, the hopes for the future, or the challenges that are perceived by the members. The ministries and programs that are developed after such an exercise is undertaken may be very different from those that were thought to be needed before the congregation looked at itself.

In planning for Christian education it is important to look at the church and its setting, to examine the beliefs of the congregation and its motivation for mission, to evaluate the existing programs, to identify the challenges or problems, and to explore the possibilities. This chapter will describe a planning strategy and demonstrate how this method could be applied in several types of congregations. As you read each section, you will find that small churches have some problems but that they also have many opportunities to minister to people and to help them live lives of faithful service.

A Strategy for Evaluation and Planning

The church board or Christian education committee of a congregation should involve itself in a regular procedure of evaluation in which programs of the church's ministry are examined. This makes possible the affirmation of work that is well done, recommitment to a goal, or the establishment of new goals. The following steps would help a committee to do such evaluation:

1. Describe the place in which the church is located. Is it a small town, a city, a suburb, a rural community? Has the population of the city or town changed since the church was established? Has the neighborhood changed since the church was begun? Has the size of the church changed in recent years? In its survey of the city or town, the committee may find that there are groups of people who are not being served by the church. Single people, young career couples, single-parent families, ethnic families, older adults, or refugees may be new groups in the population. Their needs may be different from those of the traditional families that the church had in mind when its education programs were first established. If the church desires to include a new group in the life of the congregation, the needs and interests of that group should be explored.

2. Make a list of the Christian education programs of the church (classes, retreats, study groups, fellowship groups). Does anyone know how and when these programs were begun? If so, list the names of the first leaders of these programs and the years in which they were involved. A look at the church register will give the committee an idea of the size of the church when all of these activities were established. A question that should now be asked is "Do we have as many leaders and participants as we once had?" If the answer is no, the committee should ask itself and the congregation if these programs are still as vital as they once were to the mission of the church. It may be time to try something different and expand the church's ministry in new directions.

3. The committee should spend a significant amount of time seeking answers to the question "What do we believe?" This will help to determine what will be taught and the way in which it will be taught. For example, if a congregation believes that the Bible is the Word of God, it will make certain that people become acquainted with the Bible and learn ways to interpret the variety of writings included in Scripture. It will want to help people to understand Scripture so that it will become God's word to them. A retreat for the church board or Christian education committee might provide an appropriate time to explore what is believed about God, Jesus Christ, the Holy Spirit, the church, and the Bible.

The reasons the church was established and the reasons it is involved in ministry could be examined. The committee could explore another question that is important to educational ministry: "What do people who live in our community need to learn about all of these beliefs, and what do they need to experience in order to live and grow as Christians?" Time should be spent in prayer and study as the committee deals with this question, for in so doing the committee will be seeking God's guidance. Often a study of Acts or of one of the letters of Paul helps people to focus on the foundations of the early church and to compare their lives and beliefs with those of the earliest Christians. When they learn of the ways that these young Christians responded to the call of God, they discover ways to respond to God's call today. When new programs are suggested, members of the committee who have been engaged in study and prayer will be able to discuss the relative merits of each in relation to God's call to mission in the community.

4. The next step is to identify the challenges and problems in order to focus on the possibilities for change or further development in the church's educational ministry. The committee may have discovered through its study of the life and mission of the church that there are too many classes and too few students and leaders. Problems with the use of space in the church building may have been identified. A new sense of mission may have emerged during the study. Perhaps some of the programs are no longer relevant to the situation, and new programs must be developed. A realization of the facts of the congregation's financial situation may suggest the need for examining the congregation's stewardship. Now the committee has something to work with and can begin making a list of suggested changes, plans, and projects.

The challenges and possibilities identified by a congregation will be related to the type of church it is and the community in which it is located. For example, a church in a small rural community might discover that its leaders are too few and too thinly spread throughout the life of the church. It would be unrealistic to think of developing more programs, but the Christian education committee could think of developing an educational ministry that is integrated into the life of the church and that takes advantage of the natural gatherings and groupings of the congregation. If the whole congregation attends Sunday church school, this might be a good time to try some learning activities that all generations can do together. From time to time, opening exercises—a traditional activity in many small church Sunday church schools—could be used for a seasonal celebration, for a dramatic production, for learning a new hymn, or to prepare for a service project.

Many of the people in the church may be learning about the Christian way of life through their contacts with others in the church and community. If living together is a way that Christians learn, then the congregation could provide programs and materials for families, business people, or fellowship groups. The church could hold occasional evening seminars for parents of young children or for couples with aging parents or for business leaders. At these gatherings people could discuss the challenges they face in life, hear a speaker, see a video, or gather helpful resources. These types of activities help people in communities to live out what they say they believe.

In many small churches children and adults attend worship together. The pastor and the education committee could work together to plan ways in which educating moments might be incorporated into the worship service. Children's sermons, sermons that help the congregation to learn more about church holidays or biblical themes, introductions to worship that explain what is going to happen in the service, introductions to the Scripture reading that explain the context, and interpretation of hymns and responses can help people to gain a better understanding of worship, Scripture, and religious expression.

Other ongoing activities of the church should be considered part of the education program. These could be supported by the education committee. The midweek Bible study group or the women's circle might appreciate suggestions about curriculum resources. Church dinners and other traditional celebrations could be enhanced by the telling of Bible stories or the singing of songs that tell the gospel message. By focusing on the life and activities of the church and finding ways to support and expand these activities, a Christian education committee will be contributing toward the development of congregational identity. Leaders in a congregation that has identified its mission and purpose will feel good about their work and have their talents affirmed.

A small church in a city might find that it has some of the same leadership problems as the rural church. However, this type of congregation, although small in numbers, often has a *large* building with *large* rooms. The preschool class may seem lost in a big room, and the teenagers don't feel comfortable in the formal arrangements of the church rooms. The church board or education committee will want to look at the ways in which the church building is used and at the history of each room before proposing any major program or space changes. It may be that the men's Bible class has been meeting in St. John Hall for fifty years or that the ladies' parlor is named after the first president of the missionary society. Rooms such as these are not appropriate places for teenagers to paint murals on the walls. When the decision is made that some rooms should be modified or that some should not be used in winter because of heating costs or that a certain group of rooms should house the church's new after-school program, the board should be ready with some transitional activities. The life of the founder for whom the room is named could be celebrated; special artifacts could be moved to a permanent display area; and the room could be rededicated for its new use. Most of our church founders wanted to see churches established so that the gospel would be proclaimed. If it is necessary to make some changes in order to carry out that mission, we must be as courageous as the founders were.

The small church in a large city or town often has ecumenical opportunities that may not exist elsewhere. If several small churches have found the numbers of participants in their education programs to be diminishing, they might benefit from cooperative educational ministries. There may be two or more congregations that work well together. These congregations could co-sponsor a Bible study series or a program for a special interest group in the city: single parents, older adults, or newcomers. They might hold vacation church school together or develop a youth ministry. This type of ecumenical cooperation often draws in those who are not involved in any church. It is enriching to individuals and encouraging to churches.

The small church in an older suburban community may discover that it is still trying to carry on all of the programs that were established during the years when the community had many young families. Now those families are grown, and there are not as many children in the church school or adults in the leadership roles. This is the church that should ask itself, "Do we need all of these groups?" If the church board will begin with the question "What is our mission?" and explore all of the potential for mission in the community, it may find that the church has been ministering to a community of the past and ignoring the community that has emerged in the church's neighborhood. There may be a limited number of children among the member families, but there may be many children in the neighborhood. The families in the neighborhood may have different interests from those of the people who developed the original programs. The church leaders may have to find ways to get out into the neighborhood to visit with people and listen to their concerns. The large education wing that was built during the postwar years might be full again if programs were held after school. Adults might attend worship, classes, or fellowship activities if these events were not confined to traditional meeting schedules. A look at the community might inspire the older suburban congregation to try many new approaches to ministry.

A small church in a new community faces challenges that are different from challenges in other churches. On the one hand, the church doesn't act small because the congregation and the denomination expect growth. The church usually tries to offer all of the programs that a large church would have. On the other hand, it is a small church with limited funds and a limited pool of leaders.

The congregation may have started out as an intergenerational fellowship, but it has changed each year as new people and new programs have been added. Such a congregation should regularly evaluate all that it does. Christian education can be an integral part of the life of the congregation if the people consider their mission: to evangelize people in a new territory. Often the people that a new church reaches are new Christians. It is easy to find out their needs and interests because the congregation is small and the pastor and church leaders know who the new people are. Many people volunteer such information when they are visited by an evangelism team.

Perhaps when they did their evaluation, the church board or education committee discovered that leadership development is a problem and a challenge for the congregation. There are so many new people that there are not enough experienced Christians to work with them. There may be few who have had contact with the particular denomination.

Encouraging interested people to participate in denominational workshops, calling upon the members of the denomination's staff to be involved in educating and planning, and calling upon experienced members of a neighboring congregation of the same denomination to help with programs are all ways to approach this challenge.

The educational ministry of a young church changes each year. Class groupings in the church school change as the number and ages of children change. Youth ministry, vacation church school, and retreats may at first be undertaken with another congregation, but soon the congregation wants to develop its own activities. The challenge for the small church in the new community is to remain faithful to God's plan for that church. It is tempting to develop too many programs too soon because "a church should have them." Leaders can become just as burned out in a growing community as they can in a small older community. Churches should avoid placing people in positions of responsibility before they are ready and offering programs before they are properly planned, staffed, and supported.

Small racial/ethnic congregations may find that their challenges are similar to those faced by other congregations in their communities, but there may also be some problems and challenges unique to the racial/ethnic churches. The primary mission is the communication of the gospel, but the congregation may also want to preserve some of the values and uniqueness of its culture. Education about the denomination may have to be included in the church's education program so that the ways of work and organization of the denomination will be familiar to the people, thus enhancing their participation in the larger family of faith. As new generations are added, the congregation may experience "generation gap" problems. The generations may have different needs, interests, and ways of doing things. This may cause disagreements among church leaders and among family members. The church may even see its younger generation searching elsewhere for meaningful activities. The congregation may need to consider the development of Christian education programs that help racial/ethnic families to discuss what is happening to their culture as it interacts with the new culture in which the family is living.

A racial/ethnic congregation might ask itself the following questions as it surveys its traditions, programs, and activities:

- What are the most important things we do?
- How do these activities help us to
  —tell the gospel story?
  —tell the story of our people?
  —tell the story of our church?
  —live a Christian life?

When these and other similar questions have been discussed, the education committee or church board will know what the church is looking for in programs, curriculum materials, and leadership. Many denominations have racial/ethnic curriculum projects that welcome such input, and often there are leadership training funds available for racial/ethnic churches.

Small churches, wherever they are, experience problems when inviting, developing, and supporting leaders. They experience disappointment when few people attend programs or events that they had hoped would draw in new people. When a church feels discouraged about this, it should remember that the education programs of the small church provide special learning experiences that should not be underestimated. The close relationships between teachers and students and the supportive atmosphere of the smaller learning groups allow people to explore faith issues in more personal and intimate ways.

Problems with the church building are common to small churches. Discussions of the building's size, condition, and amount of debt are frequently heard at board meetings. The church budget and the stewardship of the congregation often determine the extent of the Christian education ministry. Curriculum costs and the expense of heating the building for a program or renting a room in the community sometimes delay a needed ministry. However, Christian education does not have to be expensive. If a congregation can look at its whole life and see that the educational dimension is present in all that it does, it can begin to strengthen those parts of each program that teach people how to live as Christians in the world.

A Quick Review of the Strategy for Evaluation and Planning

- Describe the place in which you live.
- List the programs and activities of your Christian education ministry, noting the number of leaders and participants.
- Explore the questions "What do we believe?" and "What beliefs do our programs reflect?"
- Identify challenges, problems, and possibilities for change and development.

Steps to Take as You Proceed with Planning

1. Be intentional about including the educational dimension in everything the church does.

2. Develop programs slowly. Take time for leader education. Do pilot projects and short-term studies to find out if programs are helpful to people. Ask the leaders and participants for suggestions, impressions, and reflections.

3. Find out what the congregation enjoys and does well

and focus on that. If church festivals are the congregation's forte, remember that the people of God told the story of their faith on festival days.

4. Be careful about what you establish; you will be surprised at how quickly traditions develop.

3

Roles of Educational Leaders

Leadership patterns in small churches are both formal and informal. The church board or Christian education committee may have formal responsibility for the church's education program, but it may be the Bible study leader or the church school superintendent who makes the real decisions about what goes on in the education program. A former church school superintendent may exert influence over some of the leaders, or the church treasurer may have the last word on the development of any new programs. It is important, therefore, to look at the organizational structure and leadership style of the church in order to find ways to support the programs of the educational ministry.

A question that should be asked at the outset is "Who makes the decisions about the church's educational ministry?" In some cases the church board plans all of the programs in the church's ministry. In such a situation, communication between program areas is easily accomplished. During the course of a single meeting members can determine whether a program will fit into the schedule, whether or not there is enough money in the treasury to do it, and who will be in charge. In other churches the Christian education committee handles these decisions. This committee meets regularly to plan, evaluate, and support the education programs. The committee brings its plans to the church board for approval and then is responsible for implementing the plans. In still other churches it may be the pastor who makes most of the decisions. The pastor will then depend upon the board or education committee to carry out the plans. Knowing what has to be done and deciding who will do it are important parts of the planning process.

The administration of the church's Christian education program involves knowledge of the tasks that must be accomplished and commitment to the goals of the program that has been established by the church. A church board, Christian education committee, or pastor should be able to communicate to the congregation the reasons for a particular program or curriculum and the criteria that were used in the selection of leaders. Knowledge of the philosophy behind the program and understanding of the hoped for outcome of the program will help the board or committee in its task of organizing and staffing.

The first thing to have in mind, then, is "Why are we carrying out this program?" All other questions and all decisions will relate to the answer of this question. For example, if the answer to the question "Why do we have a church school?" is "So that children, youth, and adults can learn the story of the faith of the people of God, have contact with today's people of God, and develop their own faith responses to God's gift of salvation in Jesus Christ," then everything the church school does should relate to this goal. Likewise, the type of curriculum selected, the leaders who are invited to serve, and the activities that are chosen should also relate to the goal.

When the goals have been established, the board or committee is ready to ask questions about the many responsibilities involved in carrying out a Christian education program. The following are some possible questions.

Who Will Design the Program?

Who will determine the number of classes or activities, select the curriculum, establish the budget, determine what is expected of the teachers and leaders, decide which rooms will be used, and determine when special events will take place? Decisions like these are often in the province of the church board. Sometimes a Christian education committee or a subcommittee of the board will make recommendations to the board. Usually the pastor will be involved in decisions, giving guidance to those who are researching curriculum, working on schedules, and deciding upon the responsibilities of the leaders.

Who Will Invite Those Who Will Serve as Leaders?

Leaders who are selected to carry out a program must agree with the goals of the program. Their enthusiasm, creativity, and dedication will make the program happen. Inviting and developing leaders is one of the most important responsibilities of the church. The group that is selected to do the inviting should understand fully the goals of the program and the jobs they are asking people to do. The pastor will usually want to be involved with this group, offering training, support, and suggestions. This concern is developed further in Chapter 4.

Who Will Take Care of the Leaders?

Will there be teachers' meetings? Will the leaders go to denominational workshops? Will other church members help with arts and crafts, refreshments, or other special things? Somebody should make sure that the teachers have everything they need. They may need supplies, training, comforting, or an occasional substitute teacher. The board may decide that a church school superintendent is needed. The pastor may also want to help with the care of leaders.

Who Takes Care of the Rooms?

The church may have a custodian, or members of the church may do the weekly cleaning. Teachers may be expected to clean their own rooms. If rooms are shared with community groups, classes will have to cooperate by sharing such things as bulletin boards and storage space and by being flexible about furniture arrangement. Sometimes there are special events that require changes in room arrangements. For instance, a class art project may need to dry for a week. Someone should be responsible for the facility, and the church's expectations of the groups using rooms should be established.

Who Keeps the Records and Pays the Bills?

There was a time when the Sunday church school was an organization separate from the church in which it met. The Sunday School, as it was called, had its own treasurer, budget, and bank account. The Sunday School offering supported the program expenses. Today most churches have incorporated the work of the Sunday church schools into their educational ministries. The church budget supports all of the Christian education programs. The church treasurer will probably pay the bills, but he or she will expect that expenditures receive approval from someone who is in charge and that accounting of expenditures be a regular activity. Many denominations require annual reports, so someone should be keeping track of attendance and leader involvement. Often the church school superintendent does this; pastors are usually interested in it; church boards should receive reports about it.

Who Orders the Curriculum and Supplies?

Once the church has selected its curriculum, someone should be appointed to order it. (See Chapter 6 for more help regarding curriculum.) Whether it be the pastor or the superintendent, the person must be told about the responsibility. This is a task that must be done regularly. There is nothing worse than beginning the church school year without curriculum. Teachers like to feel that the church is supporting them in their task, and curriculum is one of the things they expect to have. Someone should also check with the teachers on a regular basis to see if they need other supplies. Many teachers will buy things on their own if nobody asks. This should be avoided for two reasons: (1) the actual cost of the education program will never be known; and (2) if the teachers resent the financial demands of the position, the church may lose these leaders.

Who Leads the Opening Exercises?

Not all churches have opening exercises. I had never seen opening exercises before I served my first parish. The church school superintendent led the exercises with the assistance of one or two music leaders. As pastor, I was never asked to lead these exercises, but I was expected to be there. As time passed, I discovered that opening exercises were an important activity for developing lay leaders. People learned to lead a song, tell a story, and talk about Jesus in front of a group. If I had led this activity, the lay leaders would not have emerged. Besides, I didn't know any of the songs!

Each church will have a different assortment of tasks in the educational ministry, and each person will have a special way of doing a job. However, there are some general ways of describing the roles of educational leaders. What follows is one way to describe these roles after observing the ways in which people in a variety of congregations have carried them out. In writing descriptions of what is expected of teachers and leaders in your education program, you might want to recall your memories of former church leaders and use your imagination as you think about the best ways to be leaders in a church education program.

The Church Board

This group of leaders plays an important role in developing the ministry of the congregation. Their dreams and visions for the life and mission of the congregation can be put into effect if they are encouraged. In some denominations the elected leaders are considered to be spiritual leaders of the congregation. Therefore, attention should be given to their spiritual growth and their continuing education and development. The board will establish goals and a philosopy of Christian education that is consistent with the theological outlook of the congregation and the denomination. The board carries out many tasks as the program of Christian education is established: budgeting, scheduling, planning, inviting people to serve, publicizing, evaluating. They also have the special privilege of appointing or commissioning leaders and giving recognition to those who serve faithfully.

The Christian Education Committee

In the church that is fortunate to have a Christian education committee, a small group of persons dedicated to Christian education carries out tasks that the board has assigned to them. They give much attention to their work: planning the budget, making curriculum suggestions, inviting the leaders to serve, scheduling the teacher/leader education, the classes, and the special events. They are an important source of support for the teachers, offering encouragement, recognition, and a collective listening ear. They want to know how the teachers like the curriculum, what the teachers need, and what it would take to get the teachers to return to do the same tasks again next year. They are always looking for ways to expand the church's education ministry. They bring suggestions to the board—a new Bible study group, a youth event with a neighboring church, a class for families—and the board takes their suggestions seriously because the committee members are the "experts" when it comes to Christian education in that particular church.

The Pastor

The pastor should play an important role in the development of the church's educational ministry. As spiritual leader and theological advisor, the pastor's outlook sets the tone for the types of programs that are planned and the types of curricula that are used. As a developer and nurturer of leaders, the pastor plays a large part in helping individuals to discover the gifts God has given them. Years ago when I was a church school teacher, a pastor visited my classroom and then called the next day to compliment me on the fine job I was doing. I didn't realize I was doing anything special until he called my attention to it. From that moment on, I knew that God had called me to be in the classroom. In many ways the pastor is a master teacher. The ways in which the pastor leads worship, meets with people, or leads a Bible study are observed by the members of the congregation. The pastor shows them how to tell the story of their faith. Sometimes the pastor has to be involved in the details of carrying out the education programs. The church may be so small that the curriculum ordering or the record keeping or the furniture arrangement is done by the pastor. The people usually appreciate this, and it helps them to know that the pastor cares about all aspects of church life.

The Church School Superintendent

Happy is the church that has a good church school superintendent. This representative of the education program knows what is going on in every class, recites the church calendar by heart, and can answer a multitude of questions. The church school superintendent also has a talent for communication. This person keeps the teachers informed of developments in church life that may affect their classes, keeps the church board informed of projects of class groups that may affect the life of the church, and keeps the congregation informed of the dates of special events, such as the church school picnic or Christmas program. The church school superintendent is also mother or father to the teachers and leaders. Often the superintendent knows of crises in the lives of these leaders before the pastor does. Obviously it is important for the pastor and the church school superintendent to have a healthy working relationship.

The Teachers

No church can have an education program without teachers and program leaders. The teachers are the ones who take the words that are written in Scripture and in curriculum manuals and bring them to life, helping the students to make sense of them and apply them to their lives. They are, above all, models for students to follow, for they demonstrate examples of Christian living. When they make mistakes, they are not afraid to admit them because their students can learn from this, too. Sometimes a church school teacher is the only friend a young person has at a particular time. The fact that someone cares about him or her often makes a big difference in that person's life. The teachers are co-workers with the education committee, the church board, and the pastor. They are good evaluators of the program, the curriculum, and the needs of the students. An important component of the education program is the support and recognition of these leaders. (See Chapter 5 for suggestions regarding support and recognition.)

Other Leaders

Some churches have church school officers who keep the records or take care of administrative tasks. Some have music leaders, arts and crafts leaders, classroom helpers, or recreation leaders. These people are a big help to the superintendent and the teachers. They also learn about leadership as they do these jobs. When all of the educational leaders are fulfilling their responsibilities and working together, it is exciting to behold. The church that has taken the time to plan the ways in which the talents of individuals can be employed in the education program and the ways in which these people will be supported in their work will have a rich experience. Members of the congregation will learn to appreciate the gifts God has given them and offer these gifts in the service of Christ.

4

Leadership Development in the Church

There are two dimensions to the focus of this chapter. First, pastors will find that one of the most productive and personally satisfying aspects of their ministries can be the work they do with members and officers of their churches to help them become growing, effective, and confident teachers and leaders. This work of leader development is essentially Christian education since it involves setting goals, identifying needs, planning programs, teaching persons, developing skills, and evaluating accomplishments. Second, the primary leaders we have in mind are those who serve as leaders and teachers in all of the groups, organizations, and classes of the church that have as their primary purpose Christian education. When we consider a process of leader development, we will be thinking about and planning for these persons.

We hope that the pastors who read this chapter will be helped to affirm that much of what they do in their work with church leaders and teachers can be perceived as Christian education. We also hope they will be able to catch a vision of some new possibilities for relating to and working with those who serve as leaders and teachers in the churches they serve. For those readers who are serving as leaders and teachers in the various educational programs of their churches, it is our desire that they identify ways that they can translate and implement in their own situations some of the principles and suggestions that are offered in what follows.

The process of leadership development in the church is composed of some very basic, dependable elements. Although we cannot write a guarantee for these elements, we can be assured of some success. In this chapter and the next we will explore five specific elements to the process of leadership development: (1) clarifying what is expected of leaders and teachers, (2) inviting persons to serve as teachers and leaders, (3) assessing the needs that persons have, (4) equipping them with the information and skills necessary to be effective leaders and teachers, and (5) providing spiritual nurture.

There is a logical sequence to the five elements, and they are all of equally high priority. However, seldom would a pastor or other key leader be able to give equal attention to all five in a given period of time, and it is unlikely that the elements would ever be approached in a step-by-step sequence from one to five. What is essential is to recognize the importance of all five elements, to distinguish the characteristics and benefits of each, and to work intentionally on each one over a period of time.

Clarify What Is Expected of Leaders

In a report by the Alban Institute regarding a study of the contributing factors to lay leader burnout (*How to Prevent Lay Leader Burnout* by Roy Oswald and Jackie McMakin), one of the factors identified was "indefinite task descriptions." Persons state over and over again that when they were asked to assume a position of leadership, it was not made clear what was expected of them in their roles as teacher, chair of a committee, advisor of a youth group, member of a task group, or leader of an organization. There are several reasons why we do not tell persons everything that is expected of them when we ask them to accept a position of leadership. We are fearful that they will say no if we tell them too much about what is involved in the position. We assume that because they have been members of the church for some time, they know what to do. In smaller churches, where a few persons are responsible for many tasks, most of the agreements about who will do what are informal so that it is not necessary to spell everything out in detail. We also assume that persons are already competent or they would not have been asked and would not have agreed to accept the responsibility for leadership. The experience of many is that these assumptions are often the cause of frustration on the part of those invited to do the job as well as those who do the inviting.

If there are no clear statements of what is expected of leaders or teachers, and they are left on their own to decide how they will function, they will make their decisions based upon any of several factors. They may consider how much time they have to give and do as much, or as little, as they can in that amount of time. They may observe what the former persons in those positions did and pattern their work after the work of their predecessors, whether or not those persons were doing the tasks satisfactorily. They may have a sense of "we always do it this way" and accept that tradition as a given without considering alternative ways to accomplish the tasks. Or, they may be very motivated to do a good job by introducing a lot of new ideas and deciding for themselves what they think should be done regardless of the expectations of others who are affected by their decisions and actions. When task descriptions are not clarified as to how teachers, youth advisors, committee chairs, and group leaders are expected to function, there are many possibilities for conflict, misunderstanding, hurt feelings, and lack of fulfillment and satisfaction.

Even in the smaller church, where persons know one another and much of the decision making is informal and by consensus, there is need to articulate what is expected of persons in the key leadership and teaching roles in the church. It is not necessary to develop job descriptions, position profiles, or covenants of agreement for each teaching and leadership position. However, there are several ways to clarify what is expected. For example, let's consider the role of the teachers in the church school. (The following process could be adapted and applied to other leader roles such as committee chairs, youth group advisors, and group leaders.) The pastor, church school superintendent, an experienced teacher, and perhaps a present or former teacher could meet two or three times over a period of several months to explore together what is expected of teachers in the church. If I were a member of this small task group, I would be wanting to discuss the following questions in order to establish some clarity and consensus regarding what is expected of those who teach in the church.

1. What is the relationship between teaching in the church school and the larger ministry of the church? How are the teachers to be helped to see that they are an important part of the total ministry of the church?
2. What kind of relationship do we want teachers to develop with those whom they teach? Do we expect them to do anything with their class members at times other than Sunday?
3. What are the characteristics or qualities of an effective teacher? Must they be members of the church?
4. How concerned are we that the teachers use the curric-

ulum that is selected by the church? How much preparation do we expect the teachers to do?

5. Will the teachers work on a team of two or three, or will they serve solo?
6. Will teachers be expected to attend any meetings or workshops?
7. Are the teachers free to utilize their own creativity and resourcefulness as they plan and implement session plans?
8. Are the teachers expected to arrange for their own substitutes, or will someone else be responsible for this?
9. How long will the teachers be expected to serve?

Most pastors, superintendents, and Christian education committee members have their own answers to these questions and evaluate what is happening on that basis. Also, the teachers themselves usually have their own answers to the questions, whether they articulate them or not. Many misunderstandings and conflicts develop because there has not been any mutual sharing about what is expected of the teachers.

As a small task group, we would discuss these questions in several meetings. We would seek to arrive at some conclusions that we could all agree were appropriate and reasonable for the teachers in our church. Then we would present our conclusions to the church officers for their consideration and affirmation. The next step would be to devise some ways to communicate our expectations regarding teaching in the church to the congregation as a whole and especially to those whom we would invite to teach. It would be helpful to develop a one-page summary of expectations that could be duplicated and shared with others. Such a statement of expectations would be used as a basis for conversation about teaching and not necessarily as a document for signing, like a contract or job description.

Invite Persons to Serve as Teachers and Leaders

Once we have clarified what is expected of teachers and leaders, we are ready to invite persons to accept those responsibilities in the church's ministry. Most persons writing or speaking about the subject of this section would speak about recruiting persons to serve. I have intentionally declined to use the word "recruiting" and instead use the word "inviting." The more I reflect on the meanings and implications of recruiting, the more I think it is an inappropriate word for us to use in this context. One day I was doing some personal brainstorming about the word "recruiting" by making lists of all the positive and negative images, experiences, and feelings that I personally associate with the word. I concluded with a list that was very short on the positive side and very long on the negative side. If I cannot associate many positive images, experiences, and feelings with recruiting or being recruited, then why should I be surprised when so many people say no when they are recruited to teach Sunday church school, to serve as an advisor to the youth group, or to work on a committee?

The process of recruiting seems to imply pressure and hard sell. The ones doing the recruiting feel the pressure to fill a vacant position, so they often approach persons without considering the best interests of the persons whom they are recruiting. The ones being recruited often feel "on the spot" and trapped. They resent being pressured into doing something that they are not sure they want to do, and they feel guilty for wanting to say no and obligated to say yes. In the smaller church where everyone knows and is known by everyone else, persons being recruited may feel even more pressure to say yes.

The process of inviting and being invited is much more compatible with the style of relationships in the smaller church, and it is much more consistent with what we understand from Scripture and theology. We read in the Old Testament of many instances where God called or invited persons to be special representatives among the people and to assume particular responsibilities for doing God's work. We read of Jesus calling persons to follow him to learn from him in order to become prepared to be his representatives when he was no longer physically present with them. The apostle Paul wrote of persons being blessed with certain gifts that enable them to serve God in special ways. Often persons feel ill equipped to do the tasks they are called to do; but they are reminded by God's word in Scripture: "I will be with you." In spite of excuses, failures, and disobedience on the part of the ones called by God, God forgives, strengthens, and empowers persons to accomplish what they thought was impossible.

The witness of Scripture provides us with a model for the way we can approach inviting persons to serve as leaders and teachers in our churches. The following process can be adapted and implemented by churches of any size but may be especially appropriate to churches with smaller memberships.

1. The first and most essential part of the process is to communicate consistently and persuasively to the whole congregation that every member is called to ministry. This communication happens in the church newsletter, in notices in the weekly bulletin, in prayers in the order of worship, in sermons, in conversations, and in the regular meetings of groups in the church. As we are baptized and become members of the church, thus declaring that we intend to live as faithful followers of Christ, we have in that act accepted the responsibility for sharing in the ministry of the body of Christ, the church. When persons are invited to accept a responsibility as teacher, youth advisor, chair or member of a committee, or church officer, they should know that what

they are being asked to do is not just another job, but a part of the church's ministry. And those doing the inviting should approach their task in the same way.

2. There are two ways to think about the task of inviting persons to serve in the various ministries of the church. One way is to focus on the positions that need to be filled. It is important to identify the needs of a position, but as important as it is to staff that position, the position itself should never take precedence over persons. When there is need for teachers or leaders, the question should be "Who of our members are best equipped to assume this responsibility?" We should focus on particular individuals and not just go through the list of names in the membership directory, making enough calls until the positions are staffed. We should focus on persons, one at a time, and think about them in terms of their gifts, interests, experiences, and present responsibilities in order to identify those who might be best suited for particular tasks. When we focus our attention on persons, we communicate a different attitude than when we focus on positions; we communicate that we are inviting them to serve in particular tasks of ministry.

3. Those who are responsible for inviting others to serve as teachers and leaders should be very personal and intentional about the act of inviting. It is demeaning both to the persons and to the tasks they are asked to do if they are approached in a lighthearted, casual way. The conversation should be more intentional than the chance meeting after worship on Sunday. If the task that one is being asked to do is important to the ministry of the church, then the task and the person must be treated with respect and dignity. For instance, when a person has been identified as a potential teacher for a particular age group, the one doing the inviting should be very intentional about setting a time to talk with the person about the task. Ordinarily the conversation would be face to face; however, when one knows another

person very well, a phone conversation would be like speaking face to face. In that conversation several important things should be shared:

- The person should know why he or she was selected to be invited.
- Whatever expectations there are for the position should be shared and discussed.
- The person should be helped to reflect on his or her gifts, interests, experiences, and needs.
- The one being invited should feel challenged by the particular invitation to ministry, but not pressured.
- If the person truly feels unable to say yes, he or she should not be made to feel guilty, but be helped to consider some other form of ministry for which she or he feels better equipped.

4. Identifying persons and inviting them to serve as teachers and leaders is a process that should be ongoing throughout the year and involving several key people. The process should not be one of responding to periodic emergencies; rather it should be a planned, intentional process that happens consistently and regularly throughout the year. New members affiliate with the church, individuals' circumstances change, and new needs arise in the church's educational program throughout the year, not always at predictable times. The pastor, a key church officer, the church school superintendent, the chair of the Christian education committee, and a longtime member who knows everyone and knows the ministry of the church (the roles of persons will vary from church to church) are all persons who could assist in the ongoing process of identifying and inviting persons to serve in the various positions of leadership in the church's educational ministry. It is not presumed that these persons are constituted as a committee that meets regularly, though they might. However, it is presumed that

these are key persons who should be in regular communication with one another about the personnel needs for Christian education in the church.

Assess the Needs of Teachers and Leaders

After someone has said yes to serving as a teacher or leader in the church's educational program, that person is not fully equipped to do the task immediately. Everyone has some needs to be responded to in order for him or her to feel ready and capable to do what is expected. Needs can be identified by several categories. There are personal needs, information needs, and skill needs. Pastors and key leaders are the ones to develop a means to assess the needs of persons and to respond to those needs in helpful ways.

Some needs are personal in terms of the attitudes, images, and feelings that persons have about their roles as teachers and leaders. After they have agreed to serve in leadership roles, many persons have second thoughts about whether or not they should have said yes in the first place. These feelings of doubt are often present after the teachers have taught several sessions of their classes or after leaders have led a meeting or two. Most new teachers and leaders encounter situations that they did not anticipate and for which they are unprepared. Within the first month or two of a person's assuming a new leadership role, someone (the pastor, church school superintendent, or key leader) should call or visit with the person for a time of informal conversation about how that person is doing and feeling about his or her responsibility. Such times of conversation provide an opportunity to accomplish several important things:

- The teacher or leader is reminded that he or she is not alone; someone does care.
- There is a chance right at the beginning of one's new

work to respond to any specific difficulties that are encountered.

- By being encouraged to share feelings, observations, and ideas, the new leader is able to verbalize what is experienced and thus work through some questions and concerns.
- The one who takes the initiative to inquire of the teacher or leader's needs may be able to respond with suggestions, encouragement, or resources that will enable that person to overcome difficulties.

In addition to personal concerns and needs, most teachers and leaders (experienced and inexperienced) have needs for gaining more information and increasing their skills in order to serve more effectively in the tasks for which they have accepted responsibility. The needs for information and skills can be identified in several ways. Through conversation an experienced teacher or leader can discern areas where others need to be provided with additional information or equipped with increased skill. The pastor and other key leaders will have many opportunities for informal observation of the ways teachers and leaders function in their respective roles and will notice areas where they have need for more information and skill to do their work better. It is not necessary to formalize this process of observation. All that is necessary is for the pastor or key leader to be alert to the observed needs of persons and, when opportunities present themselves in the future, to respond to persons with help that will meet their needs. In addition to conversation and observation, it is possible to devise an uncomplicated needs assessment form that teachers and leaders could fill out in order to express what they see as their needs. A sample of such a form is presented, but in a given situation it would be adapted and revised in order to be appropriate for those who will be completing it.

Identifying My Needs as a Teacher

Instructions:

Read the following items. Think of your own needs as a church school teacher. If you have a **great** need in an area mark it with a **2**; if you have **some** need mark it with a **1**; if you feel that you have **no** need in an area then mark it with a **0**.

In order to be a more effective teacher I need:

to understand more about the persons I teach   _____

help in using the curriculum that is provided   _____

the opportunity to study with other adults   _____

guidelines to help me in planning lessons   _____

skill in using the Bible and Bible study tools   _____

help in asking questions and leading discussions   _____

to know more about how to use audiovisuals   _____

to know more about how to use music and art   _____

more skill in telling stories   _____

suggestions about dealing with behavior problems   _____

skill in using the Bible with the students   _____

other (state this need explicitly)_____

5

Equipping and Nurturing Educational Leaders

In chapter four we identified three important elements of a process for developing teachers and leaders in Christian education. We emphasized the value of clarifying what is expected of those who will be responsible for the classes and groups of the church. We made a big point of the difference between inviting persons to teach or lead and recruiting them. And we stressed the importance of assessing the needs that persons have so that they will be able to accomplish what they have been invited to do. In this chapter we will focus on the fourth and fifth elements in the process of developing teachers and leaders: equipping them with information and skills and providing spiritual nurture.

Equip Teachers and Leaders with Information and Skills

Once the teachers' and leaders' needs for information and skills have been determined, it is possible to respond to many of those needs with specific strategies that will equip them to do their work more effectively. We are speaking of equipping persons rather than training them because persons need more than training when they are faced with doing a job. They need nurture and support that come from sources other than training strategies. One of the best ways to equip persons to accomplish their tasks is to provide a class or a workshop. Even though classes and workshops are excellent ways to equip persons with information and skills, these events are not always the best strategies to use in the church with a small membership where the potential number of participants in a class or workshop would be relatively few.

However, it is possible to cooperate with other churches in the community to sponsor a class or workshop to which all teachers or leaders would be invited. Such cooperative workshops focus on information and/or skills that are relevant to all participants regardless of the curriculum they are using or their denominational affiliation. For instance, a workshop featuring "The Art of Asking Questions" could be a valuable workshop for the teachers of all age groups and all churches. Or a workshop for all committee chairpersons could focus on the topic "Planning and Leading Meetings." The skills necessary for leading meetings are somewhat generic. Therefore, no matter what the committee's task or focus, a leader can benefit from developing some very basic skills, such as preparing an agenda, delegating responsibilities, making decisions, and communicating with others. Consider the following factors when planning such workshops.

- Arrange for a leader who is skilled in the subject matter and who will plan for maximum involvement of the participants rather than just speak about the subject.
- Promote the workshop with clear, inviting information so that prospective participants will know what to expect and how they might benefit from attending.

- Target the workshop invitations to persons who have the particular needs being addressed.
- Provide opportunity for participants to interact with one another as well as with the leader.
- Plan time for the participants to practice the skill or discuss the information that is the focus of the workshop.
- Prepare in advance one or more pages of a handout that summarizes important points of the workshop, includes suggestions of "how to do it," or recommends particular resources.
- Arrange the space where the workshop is held so that it is inviting and comfortable. Light refreshments add to the comfort level.
- Sitting at tables will ordinarily be more conducive to a successful workshop than sitting in a circle of folding chairs.

Such workshops would not only equip persons with skills and information but also provide a significant measure of nurture and support.

There are at least three other resources, in addition to classes and workshops, that may be especially appropriate for equipping the teachers and leaders in churches with smaller membership: (1) books and periodicals, (2) experienced friends, and (3) briefing sessions. **Books and periodicals** addressing teachers and leaders in Christian education and featuring subjects that would be helpful to them are plentiful and are a way to provide information. Often there are articles that focus on specific skills. It is not feasible for every teacher or leader to subscribe to a periodical or to purchase several books. However, there could be funds in a church's Christian education budget designated for subscriptions to two or three periodicals and for the purchase of two or three books each year. The most likely persons to choose these periodicals or books are the pastor and one or more other persons who are aware of the needs of many of the teachers and leaders and who are interested in reading and sharing information about Christian education topics. After scanning the resources each month, they will be able to share particular articles or chapters with individuals whom they have determined will benefit most from reading them.

There are times when an **experienced friend** may be the most valued resource for equipping an inexperienced teacher or leader. The friend may be a member of the same church or a different one; in either instance the value would be the same. Many persons who agree to serve as teachers or leaders are already well acquainted with others who have done the same task before. I think that a pastor could be intentional about encouraging persons to contact friends to seek counsel and support as they begin serving in new positions. There are even times when it would be appropriate for a pastor to serve as "matchmaker" in order to bring two persons together so that the more experienced one may give support to the one with less experience.

I remember two specific situations where such a strategy worked very well. In one church the new church school superintendent had a friend who had served several years as superintendent of another church's Sunday school. Even before accepting the position, she contacted her friend to learn about the responsibilities involved. As she began her work, she met with her friend regularly in order to talk about situations that she encountered and concerns that she had about her work.

In a second situation a young father agreed to teach an elementary class in the church school. He had had no previous experience other than his own infrequent childhood attendance at church school. Since he had a son in the class, he was highly motivated to do a good job. He realized he needed help and decided to contact another member of the church who was a fifth grade teacher in the public school in the community. This teacher was not only flattered by being asked for advice but also challenged to help this new church school teacher. After a period of time the two men became friends who shared other interests. The public school teacher did not feel able to commit the time to teach regularly on Sundays but felt challenged and gratified to be able to help someone else. The inexperienced church school teacher learned about the abilities, interests, and needs of children. He learned what to expect of the age group he was teaching and what kinds of activities worked best.

In both of these situations there was no formal planning or structure to facilitate the arrangements of the persons contacting and meeting each other. The initiative of the inexperienced persons caused it to happen. However, with just a little planning and thinking ahead, there are many others who could be helped if someone would suggest the possibility to them or perhaps provide some names of persons with experience who might be willing to be consultants to them as they begin their new responsibilities.

A briefing session is a meeting conducted by a pastor, church school superintendent, experienced teacher, or other key leader for one or more other teachers or leaders in order to help them prepare for classes they will teach or meetings they will lead. Briefing sessions are helpful strategies for both experienced and inexperienced teachers and leaders. For example, a pastor could meet with the chairperson of the Christian education committee several days or a week prior to a meeting of the committee. Even though there may be only three to six persons on the committee and they may know one another well, it is still important to plan a meeting carefully so that issues can be explored, programs planned, and decisions made. With such preparation those who attend will feel that it has been worth their time, that something really was accomplished. At the briefing session, which will be about an hour, there are several types of things that will be explored.

- How does the chairperson feel about what was accomplished at the last meeting?
- What is a topic and an appropriate Bible passage that could serve as a focus for the opening devotions that will help members recognize more clearly the nature of the educational ministry of the church?
- What are the most important items to be discussed at the meeting? What are the issues (time, persons, budget, and so forth) present in those items?
- If there are members of the committee who are not following through on their responsibilities, how can we help them?
- What programs will be happening several months from now that we should anticipate and for which we should do some preliminary planning?

A briefing session for teachers would have a different purpose and focus but would be just as valuable. In one particular church school the superintendent meets once a month with each of the four teams of teachers (preschool, younger elementary, older elementary, and youth). These meetings are not just to do the initial planning for the next month's lessons. She meets for about an hour and a half with each team at a time and place convenient to everyone. Over the course of the months they do a number of things together.

- They do some Bible study at an adult level for their own nurture on a subject that will be covered in one or more of the coming lessons.
- They discuss the needs of particular students and ways to respond to them.
- They review one or two resources that are recommended in the curriculum to be used in next month's lessons.
- They share with one another ideas and resources they have that might supplement what is suggested in the curriculum.
- They discuss theological and biblical questions in order to develop some clarity in their own minds before they deal with the subject with the children.
- And, they pray together—for themselves, for the children they teach, for the ministry of their church, and for whatever else is a need or concern of those present.

Briefing sessions not only provide persons with more knowledge and skills to be better equipped to lead a meeting or teach a class; they also contribute to the building of community and the nurturing of relationships among those who are present and working together on a shared task.

Along with classes, workshops, books and periodicals, experienced friends, and briefing sessions, there are other strategies that are helpful for equipping leaders and teachers. Retreats that include time for study and worship, one-week summer conferences for leadership development, videocassettes featuring Christian education subjects, observation of others teaching classes or leading meetings, and case studies for discussion of educational matters—all have potential for equipping teachers and leaders with the knowledge and skills necessary to enable them to serve effectively. All of the strategies are not equally beneficial to every person. Depending upon one's needs, interests, learning style, and time available, one strategy will be more appropriate for one person and another strategy for a second person. It is important to consider a variety of strategies and try to match the ones that fit different persons.

Nurture Teachers and Leaders Spiritually

In addition and in some ways even more important to equipping persons with knowledge and skills is nurturing and supporting them spiritually. They need such nurture and support, not because they are leaders and teachers, but because they are children of God, created in the image of God and called by God to serve as faithful members in the ministry of the church. To fulfill their calling, they must receive continual nurture and support in and through all they do to serve God. Spiritual growth and learning happen when persons are invited to reflect on their own life journeys and to share their experiences with others in an accepting, caring, and trusting environment. Persons are helped to grow spiritually when they open themselves to God and one another through prayer, reading Scripture, singing, speaking, and reflecting. Spiritual growth is one of the primary goals of Christian ministry in general and Christian education in particular. Spiritual growth is an illusive term that has many diverse meanings. I see spiritual growth as being what the apostle Paul expressed when he wrote,

". . . some [are called] to be pastors and teachers, to prepare God's people for works of service, so that the body of Christ may be built up, until we all reach unity in the faith and in the knowledge of the Son of God and become mature, attaining to the whole measure of the fullness of Christ" (Ephesians 4:11–13, NIV).

This kind of growth cannot be measured on a chart or scale, nor can it be described in precise ways that can be applied identically to every person. However, persons are nurtured through corporate activities such as worship, study, meetings, fellowship groups, and service projects. And individuals are nurtured personally through prayer, reading Scripture, meditation, writing in journals, conversation with friends, and reflection on readings. Such corporate and individual activities lead persons to become more aware of their relationship with God and with the people of God and more discerning of their own gifts, needs, hurts, joys, and opportunities for service to others. Such growth leads to living faithfully as ones called by God for ministry in, through, and beyond the church on behalf of all creation.

Pastors, teachers, and leaders are the ones who are able to help set the stage, to provide the models, and to offer the possibilities for spiritual growth to occur within persons and groups of the church. In order for this to happen, several factors must be considered and planned for.

- There needs to be **time**. It takes more than a brief prayer to open a meeting or class. If part of the order of creation is six days for labor and one day for sabbath, then perhaps an appropriate balance of time in a two-hour meeting would be 15–20 minutes for "sabbath" and 100–105 minutes for work. The "sabbath time" would be spent in prayer, Bible study, and/or personal sharing. (See the example that follows for an illustration of what is intended here.)

- There needs to be **structure**. For the time to be well spent and of value to the participants, someone must plan ahead and be able to give guidance to the process. Structure need not imply rigidity. What it does imply is that someone has cared enough to plan ahead, to think through a process that leads persons in the group to spend a few moments sharing together who they are in relation to God and to one another and where they are in their journey of faith.

- There needs to be an environment of **acceptance and trust**. Persons will not share their feelings, their doubts, their beliefs, and their hopes unless they are confident that others in the group will be accepting and supportive of who and where they are in their journeys at that time. In spiritual growth there are not necessarily any experts. No one has all of the answers. No one's questions are inappropriate. No one can declare that he or she has "arrived" at the maximum level of growth. Rather, everyone has embarked upon a journey and is traveling along the way. Some may have encountered fewer obstacles. Some may have proceeded farther along the way. And some may have lost their way temporarily. However, everyone on the journey needs the encouragement and support of all the others.

- And, there needs to be **commitment**. Pastors, teachers, and leaders need to be committed to spiritual growth as a high priority. Members of groups, classes, and the worshiping congregation need to be committed to the desire for spiritual growth. Together leaders and members must be committed to the reality that the time spent together sharing their experiences of the faith and life are not an extra element of the meeting, but a central element.

It is not enough just to get the job done in the service project or cover all the agenda items in a meeting or accomplish all of the objectives of a session plan or conduct an orderly worship service, as important as these are. All will be of little value in the end if persons have not been invited to make choices, challenged to commit themselves to significant actions, encouraged to be in dialogue with one another, and nurtured and nourished to grow spiritually.

What follows is one example of a way to implement the educational principles that we discussed in Chapter 4 and to provide time for spiritual nurture in a meeting through reading the Bible and praying together. In this scenario the pastor is leading a meeting of church officers or an officer is leading a committee meeting. It is customary to open the meeting with prayer—usually a brief prayer offered by the leader. The prayer may be spoken from the heart, and some who hear it may feel connected to the words. However, there is another strategy that will take three or four minutes longer but which will enable everyone present to make the opening prayer his or her own prayer.

This process has worked in meetings with three or four others, in classes with a dozen folks present, in Sunday morning worship, and in large meetings with more than one hundred participants. The process outline below has worked without fail every time it has been used, and some who have experienced the process have shared it with others in meetings they have led, with similar success.

The Psalms provide a rich resource for guiding our prayers. Consider the words of Psalm 63:1–5 from the Today's English Version *(The Good News Bible)* as the words of the prayer. I refer to this activity as "praying with the psalmist." The words of the psalm are:

> O God, you are my God,
>   and I long for you.
> My whole being desires you;
>   like a dry, worn-out, and waterless land,
>   my soul is thirsty for you.
> Let me see you in the sanctuary;
>   let me see how mighty and glorious you are.
> Your constant love is better than life itself,
>   and so I will praise you.
> I will give you thanks as long as I live;
>   I will raise my hands to you in prayer.

My soul will feast and be satisfied,
and I will sing glad songs of praise to you.

The leader begins by stating that the group is going to share a prayer and then invites persons to follow the directions to experience a time of prayer. This psalmist's prayer is centuries old, yet it expresses some of the beliefs and feelings that we have today. The following six simple steps are taken slowly and prayerfully.

1. The leader invites persons to a time of prayer and then reads Psalm 63:1–5 one line at a time as the participants repeat the same line.
2. Each individual is then invited to select one phrase or line of the five verses to be his or her focus for the next few minutes. (It is necessary to have the words of the psalm available in Bibles or printed out so that everyone has the same translation.)
3. When each person has selected a phrase or line, he or she is instructed to memorize it.
4. Participants close their eyes and repeat their phrases or lines silently and prayerfully a number of times.
5. After a minute or more of silence, they are invited to speak the phrase or line aloud, one person at a time. They are told that it is okay to repeat a phrase or line that someone else has spoken.
6. When several of the persons have spoken their words of prayer, the group is then invited to pray the psalm in unison.

At the conclusion of the unison reading, if there is time and the setting is appropriate, participants are invited to reflect on the experience for a few minutes. In this activity of praying with the psalmist, everyone has participated, each participant has made several choices, there has been opportunity to relate one's personal experience to the psalm, and there has been dialogue, first with God and then briefly with one another. Many persons have shared their own observations that these few minutes spent at the beginning of meetings and class sessions are very important to them; they come anticipating that they will receive something for their own spiritual nurture.

It is not sufficient that teachers and leaders work hard and do a good job. Many do just that; they work hard and do a very good job for a period of time. Then they feel so empty, tired, and overextended that when asked to serve another year or another term or to assume another responsibility, they finally get enough courage to say no. When persons give of themselves—their time, energy, and commitment—there is a limit to how much they can give before there is nothing left. There must be regular opportunities for "sabbath time," for spiritual renewal, for restoration of energy, for recommitment of one's self to God and to ministry in order for teachers and leaders to continue to learn and grow in their service to God and to their sisters and brothers in Christ. By giving attention to the importance of the spiritual aspect of leadership and ministry, persons will become not only better equipped for ministry but also empowered by God to be God's own servants and ambassadors in service to all humankind for building up the kingdom of God to establish peace and justice in the world.

6

Selecting, Adapting, and Using Curriculum

One question often asked by persons involved in Christian education is "Which do you think is the best church school curriculum; which one would you recommend for our church?" That question cannot be answered quickly and directly. There really is no way to give the same answer to everyone who asks the question. The circumstances of each church are so unique that one must know something about the church before even attempting to offer a recommendation. Therefore, we will not be able to provide any quick solutions to the curriculum problems faced by pastors, teachers, and education leaders in the church.

However, we will address several important questions related to the issue of curriculum. What is curriculum, anyway, and how important is it? Who should decide which curriculum to use, and on what basis does one make the decision? What criteria are helpful when making curriculum choices? Since most curriculum seems to be written for larger churches with larger classes and programs, how can curriculum be adapted for the unique local situation of a smaller church? And what are some steps to keep in mind when using curriculum?

If one were to spend a few minutes brainstorming what comes to mind when the word "curriculum" is mentioned, a number of words and phrases would come quickly to mind—"teacher's manual," "pupil's workbook," "teaching plan," "quarterlies," "resources for teachers," and so forth—all of which usually imply published, printed materials. That is one way to view curriculum and the way we will often be using the term in this chapter. However, that is a very limiting view of curriculum. A very helpful definition of curriculum is one offered by Dr. D. Campbell Wyckoff, professor emeritus of Christian education at Princeton Theological Seminary in his book *Theory and Design of Christian Education Curriculum* (Philadelphia: Westminster Press, 1961). Dr. Wyckoff suggests that curriculum is "a carefully devised means of communication used by the church in its teaching ministry in order that the Christian faith and life may be known, accepted, and lived." This definition does not automatically presume that we use printed materials, classes, teachers, or any of the other things usually associated with curriculum.

When we look carefully at each word and phrase of Wyckoff's definition, we come to appreciate much more the importance of this view of curriculum. *Carefully devised* suggests that someone has spent time and energy thinking, designing, and planning whatever the curriculum will become. *Means of communication* states that the intent of curriculum is to engage persons in dialogue with one another, not exclusively in structured, formal classrooms. *Used by the church* refers to the whole church, all of its members, the church corporate as the living body of Christ. The phrase *in its teaching ministry* includes all of those activities and programs that feature instruction and nurture as important elements for equipping persons to be servants of God, disciples of Jesus Christ. *In order that the Christian faith and life may be known, accepted, and lived* describes the content and the purpose of the church's teaching ministry. It is not just a matter of learning some information about the Bible or Jesus, nor just a matter of stating what one believes. Rather, it is essentially putting into practice and living one's life as an expression of what one knows and believes. This view of curriculum is equally appropriate for churches of all sizes.

When pastors, teachers, and educational leaders in the church plan and work more carefully and intentionally at developing curriculum as defined by Wyckoff, they will experience more satisfaction and success regarding the ministry of Christian education in their churches. They will have a sense of direction and a basis on which to evaluate what they are doing and accomplishing. They will raise to higher visibility and priority the place of teaching in the total ministry of the church. And they will be concerned about the relation of Christian education to the total ministry of the church.

In the course of a year in the church, many pastors and education leaders will experience one or more of the following situations, all of which are indicative of issues related to curriculum evaluation, selection, and utilization.

- Some of the teachers are unhappy with the printed resources that have been selected for them to use in their classes.
- Teachers are using the curriculum ineffectively either because they don't understand it or because they do not spend enough time planning to use it.
- There are teachers and parents who want curriculum with "more Bible." (What they usually mean is that they want the Bible presented differently from how it is presented in the current curriculum.)
- Some teachers have visited a nearby Bible bookstore

and have purchased their own materials to use with their students.

- The pastor is planning for the next new members' class and is trying to decide which topics and concerns to deal with in the four hours that are scheduled.
- A curriculum sales representative has called (or ads and other literature have come in the mail), offering a curriculum that promises to solve the church's educational problems better than anything else available.
- The Christian education committee or a teacher of adults inquires about a resource that would be recommended for a study group during Lent.

What is needed to respond to these concerns is a sense of direction, the affirmation of some basic goals for Christian education, and a recognition that curriculum involves more than ordering materials for teachers.

To develop "a carefully devised means of communication used by the church in its teaching ministry in order that the Christian faith and life may be known, accepted, and lived," it is necessary to engage in a process that will produce the desired results. The process can be simple or complicated; the important matter is that there be a planned, structured process that enables the church to devise its curriculum strategy. The process outlined below can be adapted to serve the needs and goals of various situations.

Step 1: The pastor, church officers, and/or educational leaders must first be convinced that it is important to set some goals and develop a strategy for the educational ministry of their church. They must also be committed to following through on the goals and plans that they establish.

Step 2: A representative task group (three to six persons) of educational leaders will meet as many times as it takes to accomplish the task. In each church the task group would have its own identity. At a minimum the pastor should be involved enough to know what is happening if he or she does not meet regularly with the group. A church school superintendent and/or a Christian education committee member would be members. It would be helpful to have an experienced church school teacher or two and perhaps a parent or two. The task group should be willing to commit itself to a minimum of five meetings and perhaps as many as ten.

Step 3: For the first several meetings the agenda would include such items as (a) discussion of carefully selected chapters of books and articles that members read to gain information and perspective on Christian education in general; (b) discussion of denominational goals, affirmations, or other statements regarding the purpose of Christian education; (c) study and reflection on selected Bible passages that offer a perspective regarding the importance of teaching; (d) evaluation of what is presently happening in Christian education in the church in light of what has been read and discussed; (e) work on articulating some specific goals for Christian education; and (f) time for prayer and personal sharing of needs and concerns. All of this discussion is intended to prime the pump in order for the task group to be able to reach a consensus so they can be more specific in terms of what they want to accomplish in and through their church's educational ministry.

Step 4: After establishing some goals for Christian education, the task group is ready to state more specific criteria that they will use to determine which programs to offer and what curriculum resources to select and use. (See an example below of goals and criteria for Christian education with children.)

Step 5: On the basis of the criteria that have been identified, the task group will be ready to apply their stated criteria to selected resources. They will be able to evaluate the resources that they are presently using as well as others that are recommended or that they discover.

Step 6: The next step is one of choosing and recommending which resources will be used, which are most appropriate for this church's Christian education program.

Step 7: The final step is to interpret the decision and assist those who will be using the resources that have been selected.

In the course of the task group's work as they are stating goals for Christian education, they may want to use an outline such as the following. In order to stay specific, the focus is on children; however, the same categories could be applied to youth and/or adults.

For example, the task group may have stated the following as their church's general goals for Christian education of children:

1. Children will learn about and be able to share the Good News of the gospel of Jesus Christ.
2. Children will take part in the common life and worship of the congregation.
3. Children will learn about prayer and develop the ability to pray.
4. Children will develop skills in reading, studying, and using the Bible and grow in their understanding of the Bible.
5. Children will grow in their understanding of the heritage of the church and gain a sense of belonging to their church.
6. Children will increase their understanding and commitment to the ministry of Jesus Christ and live as his disciples.

I think that these six goals are worthy of pursuit, and there are very few who would disagree with the validity of such goals. However, the goals are very general and must be made more specific in order to be helpful to a group that is evaluating and selecting resources. In the space of this chapter we cannot develop specific objectives for each of this six goals, but to illustrate the process, we can focus on one of the goals in order to show how it can be developed. For example, let's work with goal 4. All we have to do to move us to make the goal more specific is to add one word, "by," and then follow up with a series of achievable objectives.

Children will develop skills in reading, studying, and using the Bible and grow in their understanding of the Bible by
- being able to find selected books, chapters, and verses with ease;
- identifying which books belong to the Old and New Testaments;
- recognizing abbreviations for the various books;
- having their own Bibles and using them regularly;
- learning to use a Bible dictionary and atlas;
- discussing questions and interpretations of selected Bible stories and passages in order to share their own ideas;
- expressing their understanding of Bible stories and passages in creative ways;
- gaining a sense of the chronological sequence of key persons and events in the Bible;
- taking the initiative to read the Bible for themselves;
- relating the stories and passages of the Bible to their own faith and life journeys.

The list would be different for each church, but for one church this list was very helpful. Even if they had not needed to select new curriculum resources for the children of the their church, the education leaders would have found that by identifying some specific goals that they wanted to accomplish with the children, they would be better able to evaluate their Christian education program. Each of the six goals would have a similar list of specific things that the children might be expected to be able to do after eight to ten years of attending church school. Also, the same process, with even the same goal statements, could be used for planning for the Christian education of youth and adults.

Once the goal statements are made specific, the next task is to identify what one would expect from a curriculum or a set of resources to help accomplish the goals. Using goal 4 and its list of specifics, a statement is developed to use as a basis for evaluating the curriculum. Consider the following as an example.

Concerning its approach to the Bible and its focus of biblical content, the curriculum should:
- present the Bible as the Word of God—the written account of humankind's relationship with God.
- present selected, representative Bible narratives and other passages that are necessary for gaining a sense of the whole story of the Bible.
- present Bible narratives in such a way that learners
  —want to remember the stories;
  —desire to read and hear more stories;
  —see some connections between the stories;
  —can identify with the stories personally.
- provide a balance between Old and New Testament passages.
- encourage learners to explore biblical passages in order to develop appropriate interpretations.
- encourage students to relate their own life situations to what they read and study in the Bible.
- provide opportunities to develop basic Bible skills:
  —locating books, chapters, and verses;
  —recognizing abbreviations of Bible books;

—identifying different types of Bible literature;
—using basic tools such as Bible dictionaries and atlases.

You will notice that these statements become the criteria by which a group can evaluate specific curriculum resources. The statements emerge from and are directly related to the goals that were articulated first. By using these criteria, one could review any number of curriculum resources and make some determination as to the extent that the curriculum would enable the church to work toward achieving its own goals for Christian education. We have focused on only one of the six goals that were suggested as sample goals, and we developed that goal with some specifics appropriate for children. The same process, with different statements, could be followed for developing specifics for the other five goals and for youth and adults. On the surface it appears to be an involved process that takes a lot of time and energy. It is an involved process, but it need not be complicated. And in the end it will give great satisfaction to those who spend time working through the process and to those who benefit from the decisions that are made on the basis of the process.

Once a church has identified for itself its goals and expectations for Christian education, it may decide that it is not necessary to select and purchase a new curriculum. Or because of limited funds, a church may decide that it is unable to afford a new curriculum. For these or other reasons, the wisest approach may be to adapt a given curriculum instead of investing in a new one. There are at least four ways to adapt curriculum.

Reuse previously purchased materials. Curriculum is published on either a quarterly or annual basis. If what was purchased and used some time earlier has been saved, it is possible to reuse those materials. Usually the problem with reusing materials is not that they are out of date, but that there are not enough learners' workbooks or other resources. A way around that problem is for teachers to create their own resources for the learners and to duplicate copies on a copier, spirit duplicator, or mimeograph machine. Teacher-prepared materials are often more effective than mass-produced materials because they are specifically related to what the teacher intends to share with a specific group of learners.

Spread the resources out over a longer period of time. Most curricula provide more possibilities for each session plan than can be accomplished in the time available. Curriculum prepared for thirteen sessions can often be extended to twenty sessions or more. The problem with this is that it takes time to sort through all the sessions to decide how to spread them out. However, the time is well worth the investment because learners are often rushed through subject matter from session to session without enough time to complete activities before moving on to the next.

Utilize the abilities, interests, and resources of gifted teachers and leaders. In every church situation there are persons who have much to offer from their own experiences and resourcefulness. Keeping the previously determined goals in mind, these persons might be willing and able to begin with a theme, a book of the Bible, or a series of passages in order to develop their own curriculum. These gifted persons will not always have the time or energy available to do such a big job. However, two or more persons can be encouraged to work together to create a curriculum for a specific situation. They should be given ample time for preparation, and they should receive supervision and guidance. What they produce should be evaluated as other resources would be, using whatever criteria have been developed.

Keep it simple and emphasize the essentials. Every good curriculum offers more material than most teachers can manage in the time-frame of a typical session plan. Sometimes teachers are overwhelmed by all of the suggestions that are presented as possibilities for including in the plan. It is important for teachers to realize that in many ways some of the more basic, simple activities that have weathered the test of time are still among the best. A well-told story and a lively conversation with a caring teacher reflecting on the story may be more memorable and contribute more to learning than many of the more colorful and complex teaching activities. A series of well-prepared questions to guide conversation and discussion will go a long way to creating a stimulating and successful church school class. Using a small collection of photographs cut from magazines could serve as the basis for reflecting on situations and needs in the world today. Teachers who enjoy sharing with others, who care deeply about those whom they teach, and who recognize the importance of building relationships and nurturing faith will find that they have readily available much of what they need to serve effectively as teachers.

In one sense even the best of published curriculum is only half written. It was written for a national market and not with a particular class in mind. It was written for large as well as small classes. It was written for experienced as well as inexperienced teachers. It was written for well-equipped as well as poorly equipped rooms. It was not written for a particular teacher with a particular group of learners meeting in a particular space. In order for that curriculum to fit a particular situation, it must be tailored to fit. The act of tailoring it to fit involves the teacher in a process of planning and adapting. Whether one is using curriculum as it is published or adapting it to fit a particular set of needs, there are six specific steps that can be taken that lead toward effective use of the curriculum.

1. Gain a sense of overview or perspective. Be clear on the goals of the series of sessions. Read the whole teacher's guide. In order to be able to communicate clearly and persuasively in a church school class, it is important for the teacher to have a sense of the whole course of study for a quarter so that he or she will be able to see the relationship between one session and another and to anticipate the need for special resources or preparations for future sessions. To share the information and interpreations of biblical passages and theological concepts, the teacher should read all of the passages for the unit or quarter and also some other resources that provide background and perspective for the teacher. It is very difficult for the teacher to feel confident in teaching biblical and theological material if the teacher hasn't gained a sense of what she or he believes about the subject being taught.

2. Consider those factors that are given and cannot be changed easily. There are several significant factors that influence the way printed curricula materials are used and received over which the teacher has very little control. If one teacher is teaching four students, the curriculum will be used quite differently from a situation in which there are two teachers and twelve learners. In order for the teacher to plan effectively, it is important to consider the students who will be present and to adapt the teaching plan to their own unique needs, interests, and abilities. The teacher has very little control over the number of students who attend and must adjust the curriculum to fit the given situation. The amount of time for the usual class session is a given and must be taken into account when the teacher is planning. Most curriculum provides more material than can be covered in one hour, and the teacher must select those activities that will serve a particular situation best. Space, furnishings, and materials available to the teacher and learners influence the use of curriculum, and the teacher must plan the teaching activities in light of what is available and not on what the curriculum might assume is available.

3. Determine as clearly as possible what you want to

communicate to the learners and what you want them to accomplish. The session plans in all teachers' manuals outline clearly the focus of each session and the goals and objectives that are intended to be accomplished. However, the subject matter, goals, and objectives are all in the words of the author and may not be expressed the way the teacher would want to express them. It is crucial for teachers to think through what is intended to be communicated in a session and to express the main ideas in their own words so that when they speak with the students, what is shared will be seen as personal, relevant, and meaningful.

4. Develop a plan. Even though the teacher's guide provides a suggested plan for each session, it is always someone else's plan until the teacher makes it her or his plan. Three ways for the teacher to affirm the plan as his or her own are (a) to make choices from among the activities and resources that are suggested; (b) to add some ideas, illustrations, or activities from the teacher's own resourcefulness; and (c) to adapt or rearrange the sequence of activities to fit the circumstances of the teacher's own experience, the needs of the learners, and the factors present in the setting.

5. Gather the resources needed. If teachers desire that learners become involved in the activities of the session, it will be necessary to have resources for the teacher and the learners to use that will enable them to explore the subject of the session and to express their ideas, feelings, and beliefs. Many different items are included under the heading of resources: Bibles, paper, pencils, books, photographs, Bible study tools, cassette tapes, and dozens of other items that could be used by teachers or students in activities that enable them to explore and express the subject of their study. There are other resources, such as the questions a teacher will ask, a guest that will be invited, an article from the local newspaper, and similar items. Usually the teacher is the only one who will know which resources are needed and available for a session, and it is the responsibility of the teacher to gather those that are necessary to help make the session a successful one.

6. Implement the plan. All the preparation is in order to share an important subject with those participants who attend. It is essential that teachers realize they are teaching persons and not lessons. A plan is very helpful in moving from one activity to another in the hour. However, the needs, concerns, and interests of the persons present are of much greater importance than any particular activity or resource that a teacher has planned to use. Teachers who have spent time planning for a session will be able to be more flexible and able to respond more comfortably to the unexpected things that invariably occur in the course of months of teaching.

There is an old saying: "If you don't know where you are going, any road will get you there." Hopefully teachers will know where they are going because they have read the curriculum, they have considered the unique circumstances of their situation, they have focused on what they want specially to share with the students, and they have developed a plan. Curriculum is not only an overall strategy for Christian education in a church; it is also particular plans that teachers implement week by week in the classes they teach. Curriculum can be a very effective tool to enable teachers to make significant contributions to the Christian learning and nurture of girls and boys and men and women in the church.

7

Facilities, Equipment, and Resources

Where shall we put the classes? Space is often a problem in the small church. Whether the small congregation has a one-room building in the country or a huge building downtown, the church board is often dealing with the question "Where will we put the classes of our education program?" The ability to find answers to this question will depend upon the congregation's willingness to look at several ways of doing Christian education. Many of us think that our education programs must look like those of the public schools in our communities. In those institutions we usually find classes of single grades or subjects housed in separate rooms. If our church buildings are built with lots of little classrooms, we feel comfortable. If we have one large room in which all activities of the church are held, we wonder how we will make suitable arrangements for our classes.

Some churches may have problems with too much space. Rooms are large and drafty and too expensive to heat in the winter. We wonder how we can create a comfortable environment for the classes of our education programs. The ability to find solutions to our space problems will depend upon our ability to look carefully at our education programs, decide what is needed, and make some changes in the ways we use rooms.

The Church That Has One Room

Small churches in rural communities often have a worship room on the main floor. Adjacent to this or downstairs at the basement level there is often a large room that is used for the church fellowship gatherings and the church school. Sometimes there is a kitchen next to this room. Some churches have only one room, which is used for worship, education, fellowship, meetings, and community gatherings. The founders of these churches were often educated in one-room schools, so the idea of separate classrooms did not occur to them. Some of these churches added partitions when separate classrooms became the style.

New churches often have only one room for education. Building costs and the cost of renting space or even the availability of space in the community affect the type of space a new church development uses. Like the small older churches, these congregations must work out some creative ways to use space.

The one-room school is not a bad idea. A few years ago many modern public schools used a style of educating called the open classroom. Several grades were housed in a building that had a large open space in which students participated in learning centers. Many churches tried this approach and found it to be an effective way of educating in their church schools. The church with one room could use this approach. A gathering place for the whole group could be created in the middle of the room or in one corner, and some centers for working in smaller groups could be placed around the room.

If separate classes are desired, the large room could be

divided into sections, either with room dividers, rugs, or furniture. If the sections have to be dismantled for worship or the church coffee hour, the education leaders should avoid anything too elaborate.

The use of other space around the building should also be explored. The adult Bible class may meet in the worship room. The church office may house another group. The church kitchen may have a table around which a group could gather, and the fellowship room may include a stage that can be used. In one church the junior high class met in the attic. They thought this was wonderful because it had previously been a place that was off limits.

There may also be space near the church building that can be used. In good weather an activity can be held outdoors. One church extended its space during vacation Bible school by setting up a tent. In some churches the nearby homes of members have been used for Bible study and church meetings.

If the church board and the education committee will use their imagination, they will discover many ways to use the available space and even to expand their space. The people in the congregation who like to build things should be contacted. They may have some creative ideas for helping to make the space more usable.

The Church with Too Many Rooms

The large downtown churches and the older suburban churches with smaller congregations often have more rooms than they can use or afford to use. Sometimes rooms are rented out to community groups; sometimes they are closed up to lower utility costs. Education leaders in these churches often have to learn to share space with other groups or to use rooms that were not originally intended for church school classes.

Churches with large rooms and small groups of students may want to consider dividing the rooms into usable segments. A class could use part of a room if some attractive room dividers were built. Or an open classroom could be created in a large room. In this type of room, one class could use various areas for different types of activities, or several age groups could use various areas for different types of activities, or several age groups could use the room, each meeting in a different area.

The kindergarten teachers of a vacation Bible school adapted a basement area into a wonderful classroom. Using a rug and room dividers, they created one space for hearing stories and another for gathering around a table. The open area was used for playing active games, building with blocks, playing with cars and trucks, and doing art activities.

A group of teachers in another church used a similar space to create an open classroom. Using rugs and tables, they used the various areas for different types of activities. At the entrance was a space to sign in and choose an activity. In one corner was a table for supplies that could be used by any group. A rug and a small book shelf in another corner provided a place to read or hear stories. A rug by the piano made a space for singing and worship. A Bible study table, an art table, and a puppet stage were placed along the sides of the room.

Another congregation divided a fellowship room into four small classrooms. They installed folding doors that divided the room into fourths when closed. Each section of the room had a cupboard into which all of the class supplies were placed at the end of the class period. The room was used for other activities during the week.

Older suburban churches often have the problem of too many little rooms. These are fine for separate age group classes, but they make larger groupings difficult. The church that wants to try interest groups or learning centers can do this in a building with many small rooms, however. A summer program was conducted in such a building, and each room was used for a different center. One large room was reserved as the place for the whole group to gather, and the small rooms were used for art, drama, Bible study, and music. Each room was arranged and decorated differently from the others, so students experienced a change of scene every time they moved.

In churches where the classes of the education program share rooms with other church and community groups, care should be taken to establish room use procedures and to provide each group with adequate storage space. This is particularly important when the groups conduct similar activities. If the preschool class shares a room with a day care center, the properties of each group will be similar. Providing separate storage facilities will avoid mix-ups.

In an urban church that shared its facility with a day school, the church provided canvas covers that were draped over the day school properties on the weekend and over the church school properties during the week. Each bulletin board was divided in half. A large piece of felt covered the church school class display during the week and was moved on the weekend to cover the day school display. The result was that each class had a bulletin board and a felt board.

What Type of Equipment Is Needed?

My first Sunday church school experience was in a small church. My teacher had three main pieces of equipment: a Bible, a chalkboard, and a flannelboard with a box of pictures. Each of us students had a chair. My teacher could tell stories better than anyone I knew. She brought this God-given talent to the classroom and was not dependent upon any fancy equipment. I think that equipment should only be purchased if it will enhance the talents of the teachers. If it will complicate the activities of the classroom or confuse the teacher or students, it will not be an enhancement. There are several basic things that make classroom life easier, and the church may want to provide them for its classes.

1. Each class needs a place to store things. Whether this is a cupboard in the room or a shelf in a cupboard down the hall, it is important that the class supplies be carefully stored from week to week. This makes them readily available for class use and also helps the person who purchases supplies to see if anything is needed. Other possibilities for storage are old suitcases and footlockers. Some churches have movable carts with wheels. Heavy cardboard file boxes or boxes with lids (the kind in which office paper is delivered) are useful for storage because they stack well. Churches that rent space and therefore move everything in and out on Sundays often provide teachers with portable containers. A plastic file box is the right size for pupils' books, teachers' materials, and basic classroom supplies.

2. Rooms that are used for education programs should have sturdy tables and chairs. Those in the church who are good at carpentry should take a look at the furniture and see if any of it needs mending or strengthening. There is nothing more frustrating than a table that wobbles back and forth, and there is nothing more dangerous than a chair with a loose leg.

3. Room dividers are helpful in churches with large rooms that are used for multiple purposes. Dividers can be made of plywood and painted bright colors. Corkboard or fiberboard covered with burlap can also be used. This allows the divider to serve as a bulletin board as well. Dividers can also be covered with carpet or soundproofing material. Whatever style you choose, care must be taken to build sturdy footings so the divider will not wobble or fall. A number of commer-

cial dividers are also available. Companies that are remodeling their offices may have used dividers available.

4. Portable bulletin boards and chalkboards are useful because they can be taken out of the room after class, thus allowing other groups to use the room. A handy size is 24 by 36 inches. It is sometimes possible to find boards that are reversible—chalkboard on one side, bulletin board on the other. It is also possible to build them. A sturdy easel with a portable or reversible board is also helpful.

5. Each class should have some basic art supplies. If they are kept in a box, an art center can be set out in a few moments. You may wish to include several types of paper, crayons, felt-tip pens, pencils, paints, brushes, glue sticks, white glue, paste, a few rulers, scissors, a paper punch, a stapler, staples, paper fasteners, paper clips, assorted stars and stickers, and some modeling clay or dough.

6. A box or closet of costumes is helpful not only for church programs but also for classroom drama.

7. If the church wishes to provide toys for the younger children, multi-use toys such as a good set of blocks should be considered. Wooden puzzles, push or pull toys, and some housekeeping toys would also be enjoyed by young children.

8. Rugs reduce noise and create warm floor areas. They are especially helpful in large rooms that house several groups.

9. A church may want to provide some audiovisual equipment. A good record player or cassette tape recorder is often helpful. Some churches have a filmstrip projector or movie projector. Many audiovisual resources are now being produced on videocassette. The church may wish to begin saving money for a television set and videocassette recorder.

10. Every church should have a good first aid kit that is kept in a central location and is available for all groups to use.

How to Get What You Need

I have never served a church that had enough money to buy all of the equipment, furnishings, or resources it wanted to have. Most churches have to develop a variety of approaches when it comes to acquiring equipment. The first approach is to make the needs known and hope someone will donate the equipment. Sometimes people respond more readily to a specific need than to a general appeal for funds.

Another way to get equipment is to go to garage sales and rummage sales. Some school districts sell older equipment, so it is important to find out about that possibility. Church supply houses and office supply companies may have occasional sales. Neighboring churches may have equipment they no longer use that they would be happy to donate, or perhaps there is some equipment that they would be willing to loan.

Members of the church may know how to build the items you need. These talented people should be contacted because often they enjoy giving this talent to the church.

Sources of Resources

Resources help the education leaders to deliver the education programs of the church. The resource in which the church makes the largest investment is the curriculum it selects and purchases. Many denominations produce curriculum materials. There are also independent publishers. Education leaders should survey the variety and take a careful look at a few types of curricula before purchasing materials. Often the regional office of the church's denomination has samples of curricula that can be borrowed by the church. Some publishers will send examination packets or samples to churches. If your denomination has a regional education staff person, you may be able to request his or her assistance in the curriculum selection process.

A primary resource for the church's education program is the Bible. It is important for each church to have a number of copies of readable versions of the Bible for use in classes and worship. Each church will go about this in its own way. Many people are not familiar or comfortable with the Bible, and the church must help them through this stage to one of familiarity with and enjoyment of the Scriptures. Encouraging people to read along while the Scripture is being read in worship or in class is a good place to start. Bibles are easily purchased through publishers, church supply houses, and the American Bible Society. Many denominations grant funds for the purchase of Bibles to churches that need financial assistance.

Many teachers like to use supplementary texts and reference books as they prepare to teach, and many students enjoy reading books that relate to the theme of the class study. Teachers' guides will often suggest certain texts in a bibliography. Sometimes the church is fortunate to have a library that includes these books. I was surprised to find some of the reference books I needed in a public library. Often the regional denominational office has a resource center from which these books can be borrowed. Publishers regularly send catalogs to churches, and sometimes there will be special offers that churches will want to consider.

Films, filmstrips, audiotapes, and videocassettes are all part of our world. Many churches enjoy using them in their education programs. Film rental companies exist in some areas, and some denominations have media services. Many denominational resource centers have films and tapes available. Sometimes the people who staff these centers present workshops where media can be previewed.

Denominational or ecumenical teachers' workshops provide excellent opportunities to explore new ways to communicate the gospel through the church's education programs. The leaders of these workshops will often share new resources or new ways to use old resources. These teacher education events also provide a source of support and fellowship as teachers meet together.

Small churches need not feel limited as they plan to carry out their education programs. All churches are challenged by their facilities, and few churches have all of the equipment they need. Resources are only useful if they are used in creative ways. Education leaders in small churches are every bit as dedicated and creative as leaders in other churches. All have been given gifts and skills to use to the glory of God, and God will work through them to touch the hearts and minds of the students.

8

Building Relationships Between Education and Worship

Several years ago I* was called to serve as organizing pastor of a new church. I saw in this assignment an opportunity to establish a congregation with an educating lifestyle. I saw no reason why education could not be part of everything the congregation did. This was an erroneous assumption, for people come into churches with ideas in mind about the way a worship service or church school or Bible study group should look and feel and be. There are plenty of people in established congregations who have these types of ideas, too. I found that, just as elsewhere, I had to work very hard to help the congregation see that Christian education, evangelism, worship, fellowship, and nurture are all related.

Over the years the congregation did begin to take advantage of opportunities to educate and learn, and a special style of worshiping and relating to God and to one another began to develop. Christian education and worship became part of every committee meeting and fellowship gathering. This was not without constant strategizing and cooperation on

*Judy McKay Walther writes this chapter out of her personal experience.

my part. I found that I constantly had to reaffirm goals and objectives and remind the congregation of our commitment to evangelism and education.

If our congregational lifestyle could have remained as it was in our beginning days, there would have been no separation between worship and education. At first services were held in homes, and all of the generations were present. There was freedom to ask questions, change seats, cuddle children, and sing off-key. There was even a time for fellowship and greeting. It is too bad that we didn't think we were really a church in that setting. We could hardly wait to be able to rent space for worship. When we did that, we decided that we needed a nursery space so that the parents could worship in quiet. Eventually we decided we needed a church school, too. Each time we rented more space, we lost a little of our original style. From the moment we moved out of homes, I found myself struggling to incorporate some of that original style into the worship service and education programs of the congregation. I found that there were some ways to do this.

The first concern I had was our style of worship. I felt that we needed the moments of closeness that we felt as we shared our concerns and our joys in our beginning days. The lives of the people were changing as they formed commitments to Christ, and they needed to acknowledge this. The people had many struggles in common, and they needed to call for God's help together. On days when the boys and girls were present, I noticed that they, too, had joys and concerns to share. They needed to be included in this praying family of faith. So, no matter how long it took, no matter how many painful moments of silence went by as people decided whether or not to make their concerns known, the "prayers of the people" were just that. We learned much about the power of prayer as weeks went by and some of the prayers of concern were answered. We would offer prayers of thanksgiving and joy and speak of God's greatness.

I wanted Scripture to be understandable to the people. I realized early that a sermon was not always the best way to do this. Many of the young adults in this new community had left the church during their high school days, and some had no previous church experience. The word "sermon" carried negative connotations for many of them. As I would begin to preach, I would notice changes in their posture, facial expressions, and overall attentiveness. I asked myself, *What makes Scripture exciting for me?* Surely I didn't begin to understand it until I heard some of the great stories of the people of God. I didn't even understand the stories until I learned something about geography and history. How could I expect the congregation to understand and enjoy Scripture if I didn't provide them with the same helps I had been given? I brought time lines and maps and passed them around during the sermon. I drew diagrams and pictures on a chalkboard, and I told stories. I found that people were very attentive to the words "Let me tell you a story." I also discovered that they became pretty good at telling stories themselves. Sometimes the Scripture was interpreted through drama, with a group of church members playing the parts.

The first education activities of the congregation were part of worship. In those days there were few children, and they were present at the service. I made a special attempt to use examples in preaching and teaching that they could understand. During the service there would be an intergenerational education experience in which the children and adults would participate in learning together. Sometimes family groups would stay together. At other times we would notice that some new groups had formed as children became comfortable with the families of their new friends. I would prepare directions for each group to follow as they explored a theological concept, a biblical theme, a life situation, or the meaning of a church holiday. It was sometimes noisy, and it didn't look like the worship services with which we were familiar, but when I looked out across the congregation to pronounce the benediction and saw happy children and adults holding beautiful works of art or thinking poetic thoughts or enjoying new friends, I knew that this congregation had been blessed by God.

As the congregation developed, Bible study groups and a formal church school were established. This gave people more time to explore the themes and issues that were important to them. Children and teachers enjoyed having classes together. The challenge was this: How can we keep some of our educating style in worship? We did this by including the children in worship during the first half of the service. We also arranged the order of worship so that the children were able to bring their gifts to God at the time of the offering and to hear the minute for mission and one of the Scripture lessons. There was also a time for children, when I invited them to the front of the room and spent some time with them. I did not see this as a time to do a cute children's sermon, but rather as a time to have a personal conversation with my young friends in the church. Sometimes we talked about the Scripture lesson we had just heard or about an event in the world or in the life of the church or about Communion or baptism. When the church family had experienced a problem or a loss, we talked about that. Sometimes we simply prayed together. The children usually had some things they wanted to tell me. When a church school class had something to share, this was the time for it. I knew that I was presenting a model for conversation with children that parents and church school teachers could follow. The whole congregation learned much about faith as they heard the children speak of the power of God in their lives.

The establishment of the church school and the selection of curriculum materials gave us something new to think about in worship. How would we help the children and adults in the classes to explore further the concepts about which they were learning? Since I was responsible for most of the content of worship, I decided that what went on in the service should be related to the themes that were being explored in the classes. I bought a set of teachers' guides for myself so that I would be familiar with the curriculum. When possible, I visited the Bible study groups so that I would know of their interests. I met with teachers and talked with them on the phone so that I would be aware of what they were planning. I found that even though I used a lectionary for preaching, the themes of the curriculum could also be explored.

As the people of the congregation learned, their faith development progressed. They found that they had something to talk about, and they looked forward to opportunities to do this. When I visited Bible study groups, I noticed that a significant amount of time was devoted to this type of discussion. Even committee meetings were becoming places to talk about one's new found faith. One day the evangelism committee decided that if people could hear some of these stories of faith journeys, we would all become stronger Christians. We began to include these testimonies in the worship service. All of the people who offered testimonies had to overcome their fear about getting up in front of the congregation. However, each testimony was warmly received, and after the service people often expressed appreciation to the persons who had shared their testimonies. More members began to tell about their own journeys. These brave church members were living examples of the change that is possible when one comes to faith in Christ. These real-life examples were easy to understand, and the congregation knew that here were persons to whom they could talk. Much of Christian education takes place by example.

We learned as we watched our parents live and work, and we continue to learn as we watch our contemporaries deal with the challenges of life.

The administration of the sacraments offered me another opportunity to teach. Explanation of the symbols, actions of the clergy, and responses of the congregation made the sacraments more meaningful. Sometimes this was done in a class, sometimes before the service began, sometimes during the sermon. The words a pastor says during the celebration of a sacrament are very important words. I took care to pray about and think about these words before each celebration. I listened to the words as I said them so that I would gain new understanding. I gave thanks to God for the gift of the sacrament. I found that the people were really paying attention to what was being said and done. I know that the Spirit of God was working in them as they sought understanding.

The efforts to bring an educating style to worship brought a new dimension to the education program of the church. With so much attention going into the planning for worship, it was not difficult for church members to understand that worship is the foundation of life in the church. Soon they began to realize that all we do in the church should relate to the worship of God. Even committee meetings are places to worship God. (See Chapter 5 for an example of worship during a meeting.) Church school classes are definitely places to worship God. Bible study classes, youth groups, fellowship gatherings, and church dinners also provide settings for worship. If the leaders of the church's education program have an orientation toward worship, then worship will be part of the program. This does not mean that every Bible study group has to become a midweek church service or that every church school has to have an opening worship service. It means that we look for opportunities to worship God as we go about our activities. A preschool teacher may encourage the children to stop and thank God while they are on a nature walk or before they enjoy a snack. As the teacher of elementary children encourages them to talk about school and the things they face in this new experience, he or she can help them to pray for God's guidance. The teacher of younger youth may encourage them to write a psalm together and offer it to God. The high school advisor may plan meaningful moments of worship as part of the program of a weekend retreat. The members of the adult class may develop a supportive prayer fellowship as they get to know one another.

The pastor's relationship with the education leaders is important in the development of an orientation toward worship. In churches that have church school and worship at the same time, the church school teachers are not able to attend worship every week. This was the case in our congregation, and I found that I had to do some special things to provide a worship experience for them. Something that was easily done was the duplication of the sermon. Copies were made for the teachers so that they could spend some time at home reading Scripture, praying, and reading the sermon. On the days we celebrated Communion, I invited the teachers to receive that sacrament after the service. Sometimes they brought their children with them, and this gave us an opportunity to teach them something about the sacrament. I sometimes met with a team of teachers for a planning session. During that meeting we spent time praying for the class, for the teachers, and for the church. There were opportunities to give pastoral care to the teachers because of the relationship we had.

Coordinating Education and Worship

The congregation that is interested in coordinating education and worship should note that there are some things you can do naturally without disrupting people's traditions, and

there are some things that take planning and careful intro-
duction in order to insure their acceptance. In the case of the
new church development it was easy to do a number of the
things we did because the people had chosen to be part of
a church that was different. I proceeded in a different man-
ner in some of the other churches that I served. The pastor
or education leaders who want to make changes should
work with the church board to develop new ideas. In making
a presentation to the board, those who wish to introduce the
idea of coordinating education and worship would be wise
to include the following:

1. Let the board know what it is you would like the
congregation to learn. Example: The congregation will learn
more about Advent.

2. Explain the activities that will involve the congregation
in learning. Example: The women's group will make a banner with Advent symbols; a family will light a candle on the
Advent wreath each week; the pastor will preach sermons
about the meaning of Advent.

3. Give the board an opportunity to suggest additional
activities. (They may be more daring than the pastor or
education leaders.)

4. Outline the way in which this plan will be carried out.
Example: The president of the women's group will organize
a work party to make the banner; the worship committee
will contact families to light the candles; the pastor will
prepare the sermons.

5. Provide a process for evaluating the experience. Example: Several church members will be given the opportunity
to respond; the education leaders will give their thoughts on
the ease or difficulty of carrying out the idea; the pastor and
worship committee will evaluate the ways in which this
changed the service.

A short-term experiment like this can give a congregation
an idea of what it might be like to do things differently.

Disruption of the usual routine is minimal, and people know that their opinions are valued if they are given a chance to express them.

Children in Worship

Those who wish to include children in worship should familiarize themselves with the needs of both children and adults. Many adults look upon worship as a time to spend quiet moments in prayer and reflection. Children would respect this wish if they knew about it, but usually all they have been told is that you are supposed to be quiet in church. A good way to find out about children is to spend some time with them in their classes and in their homes. Through such an experience, one will find that the world looks very different to a child who is three feet tall than to an adult. Here are some things to remember about children in worship.

1. Children are shorter in height than the rest of the congregation. Some can't see over the back of the pews in front of them when they stand up. If parents hold the hymn books at an adult level, the children can't see the words. Even though most of the congregation stands to sing a hymn, it might be all right for parents and children to sit together and sing. One of the mothers in our congregation used to sing the words right into her child's ear so he would really hear what the congregation was singing about.

2. The Bible is a special book, and most children know this. It is important that children see and hear people reading the Bible. Showing them the page on which the Scripture reading begins and letting them follow along as it is read is an important learning activity.

3. Children believe in God and know that God hears their prayers. If it is the custom of the congregation to kneel for prayer, children should be taught to do this. If the congrega-

tion voices prayer concerns, children should be made aware that their prayer concerns can be included, too. If the congregation spends time in silent prayer, children should be taught that this is a time for them to pray quietly to God.

4. Children can't sit still for long periods of time. In planning the order of worship, the pastor should alternate periods of sitting, standing, and moving around. On occasion I would pause in the order of worship and allow children to stand up and shake out some of their restlessness. I don't know whether this helped or whether the fact that they knew that I knew they were getting tired helped, but it usually added a few more minutes to their attention span.

5. If we say that children are part of the church, we have to let them do some of the things adults do. Children like to be ushers and greeters; they even like to sing in the choir. Letting family groups carry out these tasks together is a way to involve children in a way that is comfortable for them. A church school class can present a Scripture reading together, or a group of friends can sing a song together. When children participate in this way, we should realize that they do it in all seriousness as an offering to God.

6. If children are present when the sermon is preached, the pastor should recognize that they are there. Examples and vocabulary used should be understandable to all present. Children will not learn to live their faith twenty-four hours a day if they are not given some real-life examples.

7. Many people think that children will be quiet in church if they are allowed to draw pictures or play with toys. After observing children in church for several years, I am of the opinion that this does not keep them quiet. It is, in fact, disruptive to hear the constant scribbling of a pencil. I often asked the children to put down all of their books and pencils so that they could join the congregation at prayer. They usually did what I asked, and they were much quieter afterward. I think that when children are given something to

entertain themselves, they think that they are not included in what the adults are doing.

8. Many people do not want to bring their children to worship because the children say they are bored. I always remember that my children used to say they were bored—in church, at picnics, at amusement parks, and at the circus! If children are invited to participate in worship, they will pay attention and become an integral part of the congregation.

The congregational life that developed as we intentionally built relationships between education and worship enriched the lives of the members and the pastor. I found my faith in God deepening as I observed the power of God working in the lives of the members and in my own life. This power gave me the courage to try something new or do something differently. A caring fellowship developed as we included all generations in the worship and work of the congregation. This is the special feature of the small church that I appreciate most. One is constantly reminded of the power and love of God because of the care the people give one another.

Suggested Reading List

Christian Education Is More Than Sunday Church School

Bowman, Locke E., Jr., *Teaching Today: The Church's First Ministry*. Philadelphia: Westminster Press, 1980.

Foster, Charles R., *Teaching in the Community of Faith*. Nashville: Abingdon Press, 1982.

Hanson, Grant W., *Foundations for the Teaching Church*. Valley Forge: Judson Press, 1986.

Developing Christian Education Where You Live

Blazier, Kenneth D., *Workbook for Planning Christian Education*. Valley Forge: Judson Press, 1983.

Carroll, Jackson W., ed., *Small Churches Are Beautiful*. New York: Harper & Row, Publishers Inc., 1977.

Dudley, Carl S., *Making the Small Church Effective*. Nashville: Abingdon Press, 1983.

Hartman, Warren J., *Five Audiences: Identifying Groups in Your Church*. Nashville: Abingdon Press, 1987.

Schaller, Lyle, *Hey, That's Our Church.* Nashville: Abingdon Press, 1975.

Schaller, Lyle, *Looking in the Mirror: Self-Appraisal in the Local Church.* Nashville: Abingdon Press, 1984.

Roles of Educational Leaders

Blazier, Kenneth D. ed., *The Teaching Church at Work.* Valley Forge: Judson Press, 1983.

Brown, Carolyn C., *Developing Christian Education in a Smaller Church.* Nashville: Abingdon Press, 1982.

Evans, David M., *The Pastor in a Teaching Church.* Valley Forge: Judson Press, 1983.

Foster, Charles R., *The Ministry of the Volunteer Teacher.* Nashville: Abingdon Press, 1982.

Knott, Garland, *Moving Toward a Strong Church School.* Nashville: Discipleship Resources, 1981.

Leadership Development in the Church

Chartier, Jan, *Developing Leadership in the Teaching Church.* Valley Forge: Judson Press, 1985.

Rusbuldt, Richard E., *Basic Leader Skills: Handbook for Church Leaders.* Valley Forge: Judson Press, 1981.

Wilson, Marlene, *How to Mobilize Church Volunteers.* Minneapolis: Augsburg Publishing House, 1983.

Equipping and Nurturing Education Leaders

Griggs, Donald L., *Basic Skills for Church Teachers.* Nashville: Abingdon Press, 1985.

Griggs, Donald L., *Teaching Teachers to Teach: A Basic Manual for Church Teachers.* Nashville: Abingdon Press, 1983.

Mulholland, M. Robert, *Shaped by the Word: The Power of Scripture in Spiritual Formation.* Nashville: The Upper Room, 1985.

Rusbuldt, Richard E., *Basic Teacher Skills: Handbook for Church School Teachers.* Valley Forge: Judson Press, 1981.

84228

Selecting, Adapting, and Using Curriculum

Griggs, Donald L., *Planning for Teaching Church School.* Valley Forge: Judson Press, 1985.

Facilities, Equipment, and Resources

Brown, Carolyn C., *Developing Christian Education in a Smaller Church.* Nashville: Abingdon Press, 1982.

Felkner, Myrtle, *Making the Church School Better.* Nashville: Discipleship Resources, 1980.

McGuirk, Donn P., *Better Media for Less Money.* National Teacher Education Program, 1972.

Building Relationships Between Education and Worship

Brusius, Ron, and Noettl, Margaret, *Family Evening Activity Devotions.* St. Louis: Concordia Publishing House, 1980.

Heusser, D-B and Phyllis, *Children as Partners in the Church.* Valley Forge: Judson Press, 1985.

Ng, David, and Thomas, Virginia, *Children in the Worshipping Community.* Atlanta: John Knox Press, 1981.

Reilly, Terry, et al., *Family Nights Throughout the Year.* St. Meinrad, Ind.: Abbey Press Printing & Publishing, 1978.

Westerhoff, John H., 3rd, *Living the Faith Community: The Church That Makes a Difference.* New York: Harper & Row, Publishers Inc., 1985.

Williams, Mel, and Brittain, Mary Ann, *Christian Education in Family Clusters.* Valley Forge: Judson Press, 1982.